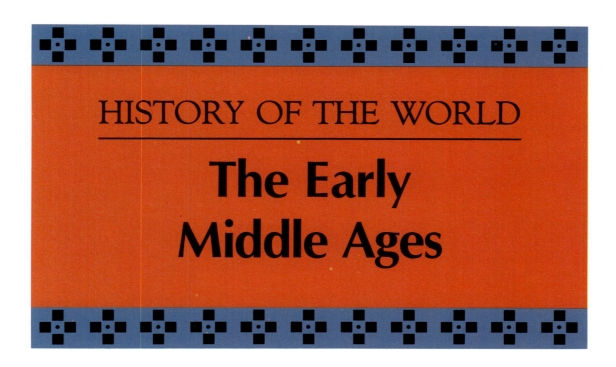

HISTORY OF THE WORLD

The Early Middle Ages

RSVP
RAINTREE
STECK-VAUGHN
PUBLISHERS
The Steck-Vaughn Company

Austin, Texas

First Steck-Vaughn Edition 1992

Italian text by Monica Dambrosio and Roberto Barbieri

Cover design by Cath Polito
Illustrations for cover and interior by Remo Berselli, and Antonio Molino

This book has been reviewed for accuracy by
Dr. Imre Bard, Chairperson
Department of History/Political Science
Chaminade University of Honolulu, Hawaii

The Splendor of the Barbarians copyright © 1989 by Editoriale Jaca Book,
Milano

English translation copyright © 1990 by Raintree Publishers Limited Partnership,
a Division of Steck-Vaughn Company.

Published in the United States by Steck-Vaughn Company.

English translation by Star Language Center

Raintree Editorial
Deborah Hufford, Editor
Thomas Pharmakis, Project Editor
Judith Smart, Editor-in-Chief

Raintree Art/Production
Suzanne Beck, Art Director
Eileen Rickey, Typesetter
Andrew Rupniewski, Production Manager

2 3 4 5 6 7 8 9 0 WO 98 97 96 95

Library of Congress Number: 90-8102

Library of Congress Cataloging-in-Publication Data

Splendore barbarico. English.
  The early Middle Ages.

  (History of the world)
  Translation of: Lo splendore barbarico.
  Summary: Surveys the history of Europe and the Middle East from the fall of
the Roman Empire to the year 1000, with emphasis on the founding and spread
of Islam and the rise and fall of the Byzantine and Carolingian empires.
  1. Middle Ages—Juvenile literature.   2. Civilization, Medieval—Juvenile
literature. [1. Middle Ages. 2. Civilization, Medieval.] I. Title. II. Series.
CB351.S6413   1990   909.07   90-8102
ISBN 0-8172-3307-5 (lib. bdg.)

TABLE OF CONTENTS

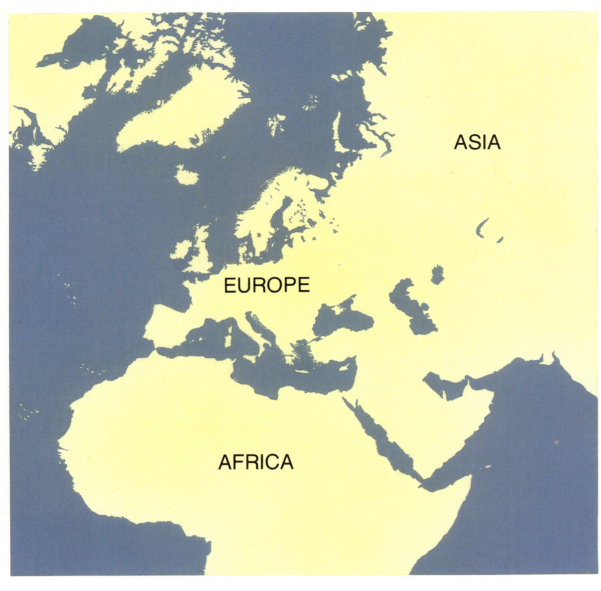

ASIA

EUROPE

AFRICA

THE SETTING

The *Middle Ages* is the name given to the span of time between the A.D. 400s and around 1500. This era is called *middle* (or *medieval,* from the words meaning "middle age" in Latin) because it is the period between the collapse of the ancient Roman Empire and the development of modern Europe. This book covers the early Middle Ages. This period began around 400, as the Roman Empire was crumbling, and ended around 1000.

Landforms, bodies of water, and climates have long played an important role in the development of civilizations. These pages show a physical map of Eurasia, the setting for the centuries of history covered in this book. The small map shows the locations of Europe, Asia, and the northern part of Africa. The physical landscape helped determine the flow of trade and cultural exchange. Mountains acted as barriers, while rivers often served as highways connecting distant regions. Across the wide grasslands north of the Black Sea, there were no natural barriers. Through this region, foreign peoples poured into Europe during the last centuries of the Roman Empire's existence.

Iceland

British Isles

Pennine Chain

Thames River

English Channel

Atlantic Ocean

Seine River

Loire River

Garonne River

Pyrenees

Douro River

Ebro River

Tagus River

Toledo

Barcelona

Guadiana River

Sierra Morena

Balearic Islands

Guadalquivir River

Strait of Gibraltar

Sierra Nevada

Atlas Mountains

Sahara

Norwegian Sea

North Sea

Scandinavian Alps

Baltic Sea

Gotland

Novgorod

Central Russian Heights

Ural Mountains

Volga River Heights

Donets River

Ural River

Elbe River

Oder River

Vistula River

Bug River

Volga River

Caspian Depression

Rhine River

Meuse River

Main River

Trier

Paris

Moselle River

Carpathian Mountains

Kiev

Dnieper River

Don River

Lyons

Alps

Rhone River

Po River

Sava River

Dniester River

Caspian Sea

Ligurian Sea

Dinaric Alps

Danube River

Black Sea

Caucasus Mountains

Corsica

Tiber River

Rome

Apennines

Adriatic Sea

Balkan Mountains

Constantinople

Pontic Mountains

Sardinia

Tyrrhenian Sea

Ionian Sea

Taurus Mountains

Euphrates River

Sicily

Aegean Sea

Cyprus

Tigris River

Mediterranean Sea

Crete

Levant Sea

Persian Gulf

Syrian Desert

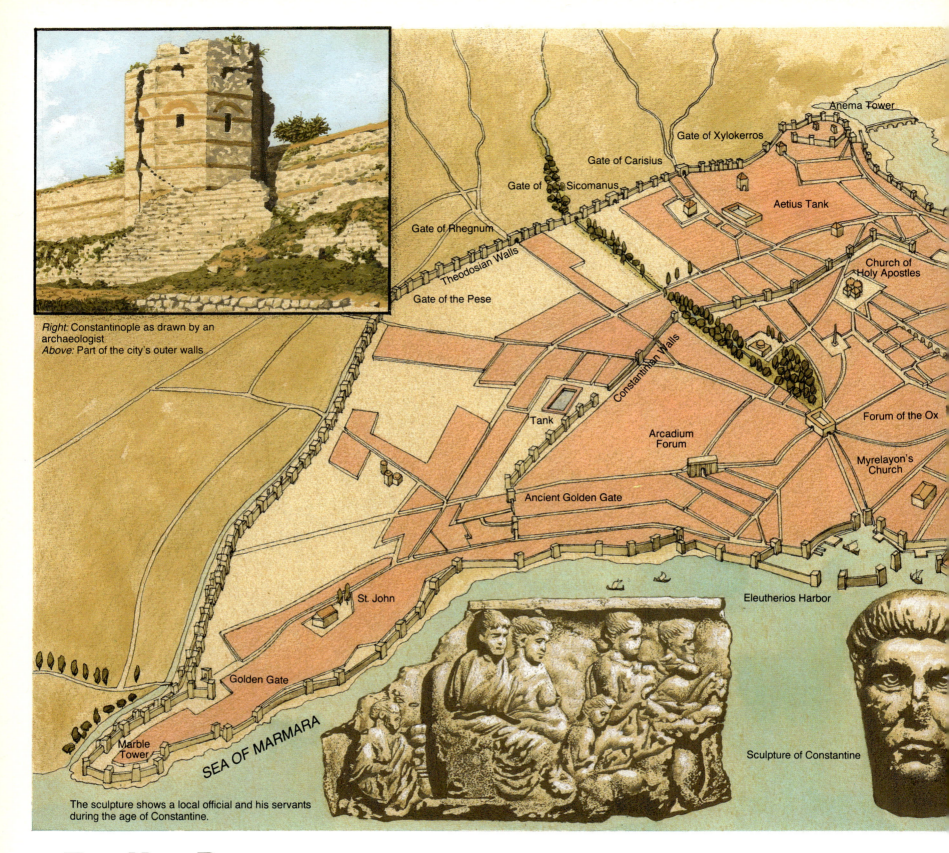

Right: Constantinople as drawn by an archaeologist
Above: Part of the city's outer walls

The sculpture shows a local official and his servants during the age of Constantine.

Anema Tower
Gate of Xylokerros
Gate of Carisius
Gate of Sicomanus
Aetius Tank
Gate of Rhegnum
Church of Holy Apostles
Theodosian Walls
Gate of the Pese
Constantinian Walls
Tank
Forum of the Ox
Arcadium Forum
Myrelayon's Church
Ancient Golden Gate
St. John
Eleutherios Harbor
Golden Gate
Marble Tower
SEA OF MARMARA
Sculpture of Constantine

THE NEW ROME

The Beginning of the End of the Roman Empire

During its long history, the ancient Roman Empire showed great skill in uniting peoples of different traditions and cultures. However, during the third century, the Roman state began to collapse from the burden of its own size. The cost of paying for the defense and administra-tion of the huge empire caused serious economic problems, so the Roman government increased taxes. Farmers who were unable to pay their taxes deserted their farms, and agricultural production fell. As production fell, there were fewer goods for the government to tax. The government began to run short of money.

The military experienced serious problems also. Soldiers who did not receive their pay on time rioted against their officers. In many parts of the empire, Rome's former enemies had been hired as soldiers. These soldiers had no loyalty to Rome. The lack of military discipline made the defense of the empire's borders weak. Attacks by barbarians (as Romans called people living outside the Roman Empire) were common during the third century. In Rome itself, the emperor's personal army—the Praetorian Guard—appointed and overthrew emperors whenever it pleased. Many Romans refused to recognize the emperors appointed by the army.

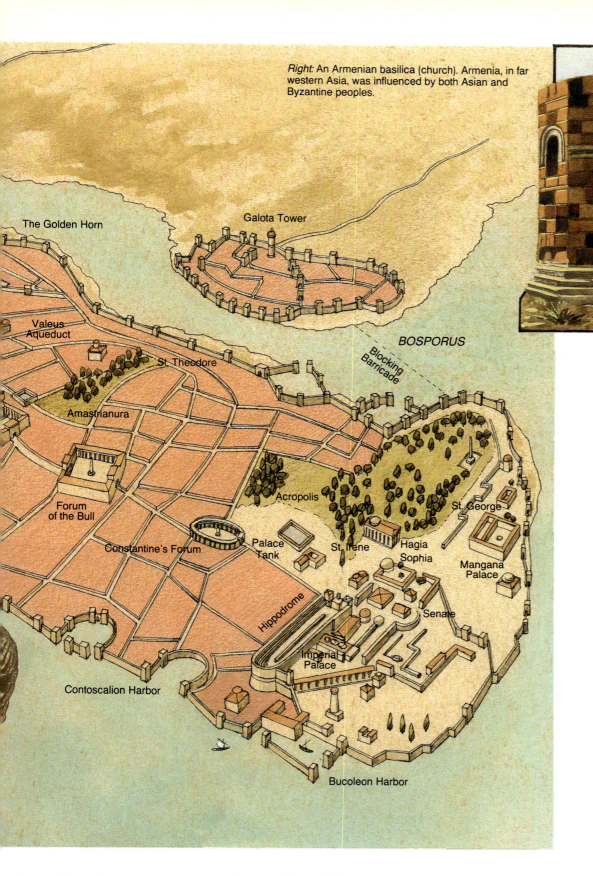

Right: An Armenian basilica (church). Armenia, in far western Asia, was influenced by both Asian and Byzantine peoples.

The Golden Horn

Galota Tower

Valeus Aqueduct

BOSPORUS

Blocking Barricade

St. Theodore

Amastrianura

Acropolis

St. George

Forum of the Bull

Constantine's Forum

Palace Tank

St. Irene

Hagia Sophia

Mangana Palace

Hippodrome

Senate

Imperial Palace

Contoscalion Harbor

Bucoleon Harbor

Sometimes there were as many as three or four emperors at the same time.

Diocletian

Diocletian was a high-ranking soldier from the Roman territory of Illyria (now part of Yugoslavia). When Diocletian became emperor in 284, he redesigned the administrative structure of the empire, dividing it into two districts—the eastern and western empires. Each empire was to be ruled by several emperors.

This system, however, led to wars between competing emperors. This divided the crumbling Roman Empire further.

Constantine

After the death of Jesus Christ around A.D. 30, his disciples began spreading his teachings throughout the Roman Empire. From about A.D. 64 to the fourth century, the Roman government persecuted the Christians. In the early 300s, Constantine the Great became the first Roman emperor to be converted to Christianity.

Constantine was the son of Constantinus Chlorus, the emperor who ruled Britain and Gaul (present-day France). When Constantinus died in 306, Constantine took over the areas ruled by his father. Constantine tried to make a peace treaty with Severus, the emperor of Italy and northern Africa. However, when Severus was murdered, Constantine declared himself to be the only emperor of the western empire. In 312 Constantine crossed the Alps and invaded Italy. On his way south to Rome, Constantine claimed to see a cross of light in the sky. Constantine thought this meant that he would be victorious if he accepted Christianity. After Constantine captured Rome, he was acclaimed as emperor of the west by the Roman Senate and the Roman people. Constantine believed that the Christian God had given him this victory, and he became a Christian. In 313 he issued the Edict (law) of Milan, which gave all persons the right to worship whatever god they wished.

In 324 Constantine went to war against Licinius, the ruler of the eastern empire. Constantine defeated Licinius and became the single ruler of a reunified Roman Empire. To honor the great emperor and his victory, the city of Byzantium was renamed *Constantinople*, meaning "city of Constantine" (now called Istanbul, located on the Bosporus strait between the Black and the Aegean seas). Here Constantine began building a great Christian city, which he called the "new Rome." The city was filled with beautiful churches and other architecture. When the empire was once again divided in the late 300s, Constantinople became the capital of the eastern empire. While the western empire fell apart and finally collapsed in 476, the eastern empire—later known as the Byzantine Empire, or Byzantium—would last until 1453.

CHRISTIANITY DURING THE FOURTH AND FIFTH CENTURIES

The First Church Councils

In 325 Roman Emperor Constantine called the first council of all church leaders. This council met in the city of Nicaea (located in present-day Turkey). The Council of Nicaea met to define church principles, called doctrine, and to organize the administration of the church. The church was divided into four administrative districts under the authority of four bishops called patriarchs. These four bishops had their residences in the cities of Rome, Constantinople, Antioch (in present-day Turkey), and Alexandria (in Egypt). The Council of Nicaea wrote the Nicaean Creed, a statement of the church's beliefs.

An idea that agrees with the church's beliefs is called an orthodoxy. An idea that disagrees with the church's beliefs is called a heresy. One of the purposes of the Nicaean Council and other early church councils was to decide which ideas were orthodox and which ideas were heretical. One question that was not decided was who should be the final judge in arguments over doctrine. The pope, who was also the bishop of Rome, claimed this right for himself. The pope held that he was the spiritual descendant of St. Peter, the first bishop of Rome, who had been Jesus' leading apostle. On this basis, the pope claimed to be the leader of the church. The bishops of Antioch and Alexandria supported the pope. However, the bishop of Constantinople believed that the emperor should have the final say over all questions of belief. The conflict of authority between pope and emperor would continue to divide the Christians of east and west, finally splitting the Christian world into two separate churches in 1054.

Orthodoxy and Heresy

According to orthodox belief, Christians believed that there was one God who was three beings—God the Father (who created the world), God the Son (Jesus Christ), and the Holy Spirit. The church taught that all these beings were eternal. The church also believed that God the Son was both God (that is, divine) and a human being named Jesus—two separate beings at the same time. Some Christians did not agree with these beliefs. These Christians were rejected by the church as heretics.

Arian Christians (followers of the Egyptian priest Arius) believed that God the Father was superior to the Son and the Holy Spirit. Many

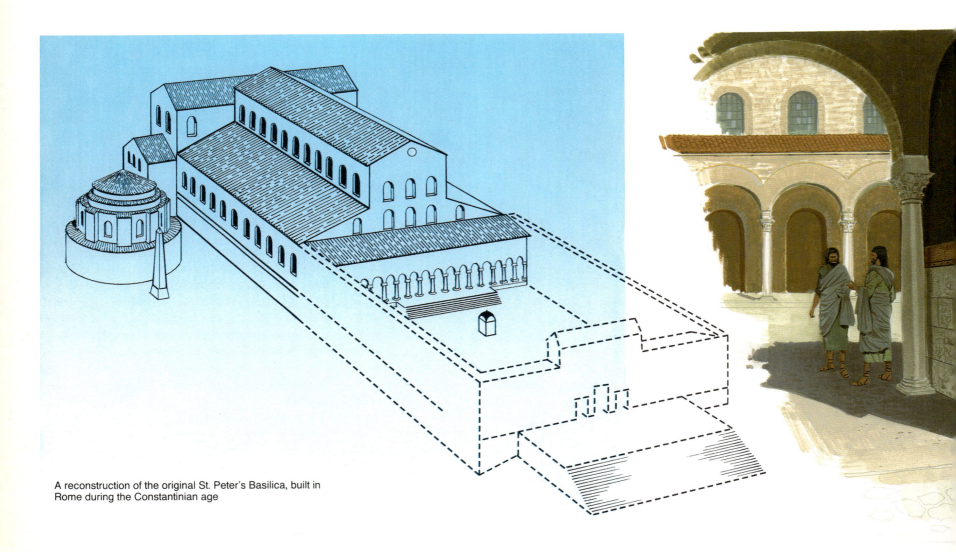

A reconstruction of the original St. Peter's Basilica, built in Rome during the Constantinian age

Germanic peoples adopted Arian Christianity.

Another offshoot of the Christian church—Monophysite Christianity—held that Jesus had only one nature, his divine nature having absorbed his human nature. Monophysitism was widespread in many parts of the Byzantine Empire.

The Early Church

In 391 Christianity was made the official religion of the Roman Empire. Temples were closed and the worship of all other gods was forbidden. While the church established itself easily in the cities, many rural people continued to worship their local gods. To help convert the countryside to Christianity, the church set up local administrative centers called parishes. The parish system allowed Christianity to reach areas far from the cities. By the time the western empire collapsed, most of its regions had been converted to Christianity.

The early church received much support from the poor. The church often gave shelter to mistreated slaves or persons accused of crimes. The church also founded charitable institutions such as hospitals and schools. Germanic invasions that took place in the 400s caused many Roman officials to flee the cities, and so the church often took over the civil government. Many church leaders were able to make peace treaties with the Germanic invaders.

Education and Culture

After the Roman Empire collapsed completely in the fifth century, Roman learning was kept alive by members of the church. The Germanic invaders destroyed many libraries, and most people no longer knew how to read and write. However, scholars employed by the church studied and made copies of Greek and Latin books. While some church officials condemned these ancient books as non-Christian, most believed that knowledge would help the church preach more effectively. Groups of scholars assembled large libraries in Italy and even in places as isolated as Ireland. During the Middle Ages, all that survived of Roman and Greek learning was saved in these libraries.

Three saints who helped define the church's philosophy and organization: Ambrose (340-397), Augustine (354-430), and John Crysostom (344-407)

Some clergymen going to a church council

THE GERMANIC INVASIONS

Under the apparent uniformity of laws and customs imposed by the Romans, the peoples of northern and central Europe shared an older culture that was very different from Roman culture. This older culture can be called Germanic culture. It belonged to peoples who originally came from the area south of the Baltic Sea. Sometime during the first century B.C., some of these peoples moved from northern Europe into central and eastern Europe. There they either forced out or intermarried with the existing population, known as the Celts.

The Germanic peoples planted rye and oats and raised oxen and hogs. Their farming techniques were primitive and quickly wore out the soil. After a few seasons—when the soil could no longer produce food—the people moved on and began farming in a new place.

Around 12 B.C., the Romans began a conquest of central Europe. By A.D. 9 the Romans occupied a large area west of the Rhine River, called Gaul (present-day France). The area east of the Rhine remained under the control of Germanic tribes.

Germanic people on both sides of the Rhine had many contacts with the Romans. Roman merchants traded finished goods such as scissors and clay jars for Germanic slaves. Many Germanic men enlisted in the Roman army. Despite these contacts, Germanic culture was not lost.

Around the beginning of the fifth century, several Germanic tribes began moving across the Rhine River into Gaul. These groups—the Vandals, the Swabians, and the Alani—were fleeing from attacks by other Germanic tribes—the Visigoths and the Ostrogoths. These two tribes were looking for new lands in central Europe. They had been driven out of their own home in eastern Europe by invaders from central Asia called Huns. As all these Germanic tribes crossed into the empire, they destroyed many of the Roman settlements in their path. Thousands of Romans lost their lives. Churches and houses were burned. Many Romans thought that the end of the world had come. Eventually, the different tribes formed permanent settlements. The western Roman empire was able to make allies of some tribes by paying gold to the leaders of these tribes. When the Huns invaded Gaul in the mid-400s, it was a combined Visigoth and Roman army that defended the western empire against this common enemy.

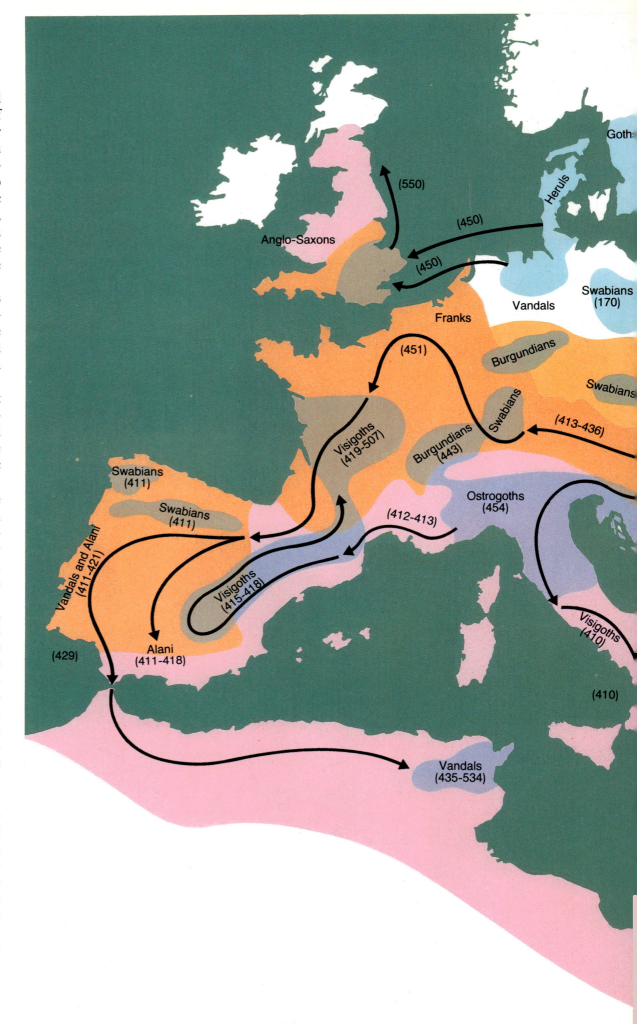

As the Roman Empire crumbled in the fifth century, invasions and migrations by many Germanic tribes increased greatly. The Huns from the east drove the Visigoths and Ostrogoths westward. In turn, these tribes forced the Vandals, Swabians, and Alani to migrate farther westward. Migrations did not only involve warriors. Entire populations, including women, children, and old people, brought their cultures to the west and greatly affected the western Roman Empire.

Burgundians
(150-250)

Goths
(150)

Gepids

Vandals
(400)

(150)

Alani
(400)

Ostrogoths
(200-375)

Huns
(375)

Huns
(434-453)

Heruls

Visigoths
(270-375)

(378)

(401)

Areas influenced
by Roman culture

Early Celtic populations

Germanic settlements

Migrations

11

THE HUNS

On the Way to Europe

The Huns originally came from central Asia. They were nomads—people who follow their herds of grazing animals from place to place. The Huns raised sheep and horses. They were excellent horse riders and spent most of their time on horseback. All year long they followed their grazing herds across the grasslands of central Asia. The Huns also hunted and lived on a diet of meat and milk. Because the Huns could not read and write, they left no records of their early history. Around 375, the Huns moved westward and occupied Persia (present-day Iran). Later, they moved into the area north of the Black Sea. The Germanic tribes living in this area were forced to flee westward to escape the Huns. The Hunnish rulers settled on the central plain of what is now Hungary—an area called Pannonia by the Romans. From Pannonia the Hunnish King Rugila launched attacks against the eastern Roman empire. These attacks stopped—at least temporarily—when Rugila died in 435. Rugila's nephews, Attila and Bleda, together ruled the Hunnish empire after Rugila's death.

Attila

By the time Attila and Bleda assumed leadership, the Huns had already changed many of their social customs. The transfer of power from Rugila to his two nephews went smoothly because the Huns had replaced their earlier tribal custom, in which each tribe governed itself, with a form of inherited kingship. However, struggles for power still occurred within the ruling family. In 445 Bleda was murdered by his brother Attila's agents. Attila then became the sole ruler of the Huns. After taking full control of his own people, Attila wanted to renew the Huns' war with the eastern empire.

Attila first attacked Constantinople. In 447 the Byzantines agreed to pay gold to Attila in exchange for Attila's promise to leave their capital in peace. However, when a new Byzantine emperor refused to give Attila any more gold, Attila turned his attention to Rome. Attila offered peace to the Romans in exchange for

Left: A portrait of Attila, done by an Italian artist in the 1500s. The devilish look shows how long the Italians remembered Attila's dreadful deeds.

An assault of the Huns on a village. The Huns were excellent horse riders and very handy with bows and arrows. Their raids terrorized eastern and western populations.

Ob River

Irtysh River

Syr Darya

Amu Darya

Amur River

Huang River

Chang River

Ganges River

Brahmaputra River

marriage to Honoria, the sister of Emperor Valentinian III. Attila also wanted half of the western empire as a wedding present. Valentinian refused. Unsuccessful with both Constantinople and Rome, Attila decided to attack the Roman territory of Gaul. Gaul was now the home of several Germanic tribes that had fled there. Attila said he wanted to punish these people, whom he claimed were runaway slaves who belonged to the Huns. In 451 Attila entered Gaul.

The governor of Gaul was the Roman general Aetius. Aetius had been a hostage in Rugila's palace as a boy, and he and the young Attila had become friends. Aetius asked for help from the Visigoths, one of the Germanic tribes that had fled from the Huns. The combined Roman-Visigoth army battled the Huns at a place near the present-day French city of Châlons-sur-Marne. More than three thousand Romans and Visigoths and six thousand Huns were killed in the battle. The Visigoth leader fell from his horse and was trampled to death by his own troops. Attila's badly beaten army was allowed to retreat. Although Aetius could have pursued and destroyed the Hunnish army, he allowed them to escape. Some people said that Aetius did not want to kill his boyhood friend. However, Aetius probably wanted to use the fear of another attack by the Huns to strengthen the alliance between Rome and the Germanic tribes in Gaul. Aetius thought these tribes were a bigger threat to the empire than the Huns were.

After his defeat in Gaul, Attila attacked Italy in 452. Because Emperor Valentinian III was afraid of Aetius's growing popularity among the Roman people, Valentinian did not send Aetius against the Huns. Instead, Pope Leo I in Rome made an agreement to pay the Huns gold in exchange for peace. Having finally succeeded in humiliating the Romans, Attila went home to Pannonia. The king of the Huns died in 453. The Roman general Aetius was murdered by agents of Emperor Valentinian in 454. When Valentinian bragged to his friends that he had killed his greatest general, he was told, "You have used your left hand to cut off your right hand."

13

THE AGE OF JUSTINIAN

Justinian

Justinian was born in 482. His uncle, Justin, took the throne of the eastern, or Byzantine, empire by force in 518. He ruled as Emperor Justin I. Justin had been a soldier all his life and had very little education. Justinian, who was well educated, became an important adviser to his uncle. When Justin died in 527, Justinian became emperor. As emperor, Justinian wanted to recapture all of the lands around the Mediterranean that had been lost by the Roman Empire. In 533 Justinian sent troops to northern Africa, where his general, Belisarius, defeated the Germanic Vandals. By 555, Sicily, Corsica, Sardinia, Italy, and southern Spain also had been brought under Byzantine rule.

However, Justinian's military campaigns in the west left Byzantium's eastern borders weakly defended. When Persia (present-day Iran) attacked Byzantium from the east, Justinian paid a large sum of gold to the Persian emperor in exchange for fifty years of peace. The combined cost of this treaty and the military actions in the west used up much of the money in the Byzantine treasury. When Justinian tried to raise more money by increasing taxes, farmers who could not afford to pay their taxes deserted their farms. Many of these farmers moved to Constantinople, where they lived on charity from the church. In addition to these economic problems, a plague (fast-spreading disease) broke out in Constantinople in the summer of 542. More than half the city's residents died in a period of four months.

Monophysitism and Theodora

Monophysitism, an offshoot of Christianity that was considered a heresy by the church, spread during the early 400s in the Byzantine territories of Egypt, Syria, and Armenia. Because the Byzantine emperor claimed to be the head of both the church and the empire, many areas expressed their opposition to the empire

Maximum expansion of the Roman Empire

Eastern Empire in 526

Eastern Empire in 565

Reconstruction of the Qaalat Serman Shrine. This shrine was built in 470 in the part of the eastern empire that is now Syria.

14

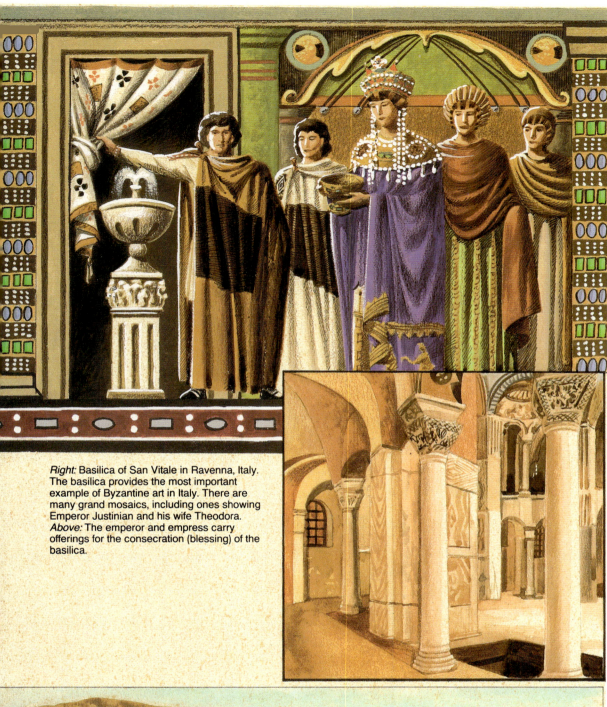

Right: Basilica of San Vitale in Ravenna, Italy. The basilica provides the most important example of Byzantine art in Italy. There are many grand mosaics, including ones showing Emperor Justinian and his wife Theodora.
Above: The emperor and empress carry offerings for the consecration (blessing) of the basilica.

Left: Qaalat Serman's present look

by adopting heretical beliefs. There was also a large Monophysite group in Constantinople itself. This group was led by Justinian's own wife, Empress Theodora. Theodora had been a dancer in the circus before marrying Justinian. Because of her humble background, Theodora was loved by the common people and hated by the Byzantine nobles. Because there were no political parties or elections in Byzantium, the people expressed their support for the followers of the emperor or empress by betting on horses in the chariot races. The supporters of Emperor Justinian and the church bet on the horses that wore blue decorations, and they called themselves the Blues. The supporters of Empress Theodora and the Monophysites bet on the horses with green decorations and called themselves the Greens. Although Theodora often opposed Justinian—and even tried to take over the government when Justinian was sick with the plague—she aided her husband in other times of crisis. When riots broke out in 532, Theodora sent her most important followers—the generals of the army—to defend Justinian against the rioters.

Corpus Juris Civilis

The most important contribution of Justinian was the *Corpus Juris Civilis* ("body of civil law," in Latin), a written collection of the empire's laws and a set of guidelines for judges to follow in making decisions. Although these laws were not adopted by the Germanic peoples of the west, Justinian's laws would be important to the later history of all Europe. Ideas from the *Corpus Juris Civilis* would be later used in writing canon law—that is, the laws that govern the church. During the eleventh century, law schools in the Italian city of Bologna would rediscover Justinian's laws. By the twelfth century, scholars educated in the law schools would bring the knowledge of Justinian's laws to every kingdom in Europe.

BYZANTIUM IN THE SEVENTH CENTURY

Heraclius

During the seventh century, Byzantine culture became increasingly separate from the culture of the west. While Greek had long been the everyday language of the Byzantine people, Latin had still been used in official documents. In the seventh century, Greek became the official language of Byzantium. Heraclius, who became Byzantine emperor in 610, ruled during the first half of the seventh century. This was a period of tremendous changes, including the birth and expansion of Islam and the shrinking of Byzantium's power. When Heraclius began his rule, the empire was already in decline. The Balkan peninsula in the north of Greece was occupied by Avars and Slavs from eastern Europe. The Persians had invaded from the east and defeated the Byzantine army at Antioch in 613. The Persians also captured Damascus and Jerusalem the following year. By 619 Egypt also had been lost to the Persians.

Because Egypt was an important grain-producing region, its loss caused food shortages in Constantinople. The economic problems that followed left Byzantium unable to pay for the services of the soldiers-for-hire that made up a large part of the imperial army. Faced with these problems, Heraclius reorganized both the government and the army. Small districts were grouped together into larger units called themes. Each theme was headed by a supreme military commander. Within the themes, farmland was given to soldiers in exchange for military service. These new soldier-farmers did not need to be paid in cash as the soldiers-for-hire did. The theme system was used first in Asia Minor (present-day Turkey). The system was later extended to Greece and the Balkans.

Near right: A representation of a Byzantine knight. The cavalry (soldiers on horseback) was essential to the imperial army's defeat of the Persians. *Far right:* The invention of "Greek fire" (flaming liquid sprayed through a tube) had an equal or even greater importance for naval defense. Because of it, the Byzantines maintained their fleet's superiority for a long time.

Right: Emperor Constantine II's coin. Grandson of and successor to Heraclius, he was one of the promoters of reform and of defense against early Arab attacks.

Amastris
Constantinople · Chrysopolis · Heraclea
Chalcedon
OPTIMATIAN THEME
Cyzicus · Nicaea · Claudiopolis
BUCELLARIAN THEME
Abydus
Sakarya River
Ancyra
OPSICIAN THEME
Dorylaeum
Lesbos
THEME OF THE AEGEAN SEA
Pergamum · Amorium
Sardis · Acroinon
Chios
Smyrna · THRACESIAN THEME · ANATOLIC THEME
THEME OF SAMOS · Ephesus
Menderes River
Iconium
CIBYRRHAEOT THEME
Cos · Attalia · Cibyra
SELEUCIAN THEME
Rhodes
Cyprus
MEDITERRANEAN SEA

16

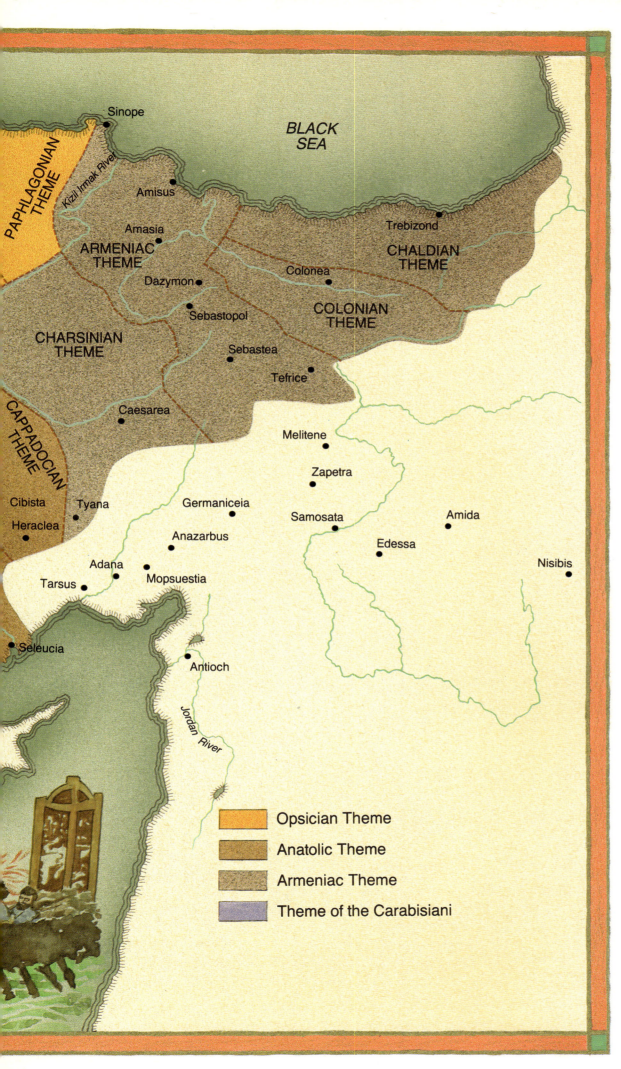

Map labels:
BLACK SEA

Sinope
Amisus
Trebizond
Amasia
ARMENIAC THEME
CHALDIAN THEME
Colonea
Dazymon
COLONIAN THEME
Sebastopol
CHARSINIAN THEME
Sebastea
Tefrice
Caesarea
Melitene
Zapetra
Cibista
Tyana
Germaniceia
Samosata
Amida
Heraclea
Anazarbus
Edessa
Adana
Mopsuestia
Nisibis
Tarsus
Seleucia
Antioch
Jordan River
Kizil Irmak River
PAPHLAGONIAN THEME
CAPPADOCIAN THEME

Legend:
Opsician Theme
Anatolic Theme
Armeniac Theme
Theme of the Carabisiani

Military Actions

In the 620s Heraclius renewed his empire's campaigns against its enemies. After making a treaty with the Avars in 621, Heraclius led his army eastward against the Persians. By 622 the Byzantines had defeated the Persian army in Armenia. The Persians were forced to abandon Asia Minor. In 627 the Byzantine army pushed deep into Persia itself. Persian Emperor Khusru II was deposed and replaced by his own son, Kavadh II. By 630 Heraclius had restored Egypt, Palestine, and western Mesopotamia (present-day Iraq) to Byzantine rule.

While Heraclius was away commanding his army in Asia Minor, Avars and Persians together attacked Constantinople. The Byzantines defeated the attackers, then not only drove out the Persians, but also destroyed the Avar kingdom in northern Greece. While the Avars were driven north, the Slavs who had accompanied the Avars from eastern Europe remained and were brought under Byzantine rule.

The Byzantine Church

Under Heraclius, the Byzantine church became more and more active in the political life of Byzantium. The church supported Heraclius's wars. Both the church and empire believed that these were wars to defend Christianity. The church loaned Heraclius money to help pay the cost of sending a Byzantine army to Asia Minor. While Heraclius was away with the army, Sergius—the patriarch of Constantinople—shared power with Heraclius's son. It was during this period, when the church shared in the government, that Constantinople successfully defended itself against the attack by Avars and Persians.

The first eastern monks lived in poverty in the desert. Their primary activity was prayer, but work also played an important role in daily life.

THE FIRST MONKS

Monks are men who live together in religious communities devoted to prayer. Nobody really knows how Christian monasticism began. Before there were formal organizations of monks, many Christians tried to live simple lives of poverty—the kind of life lived by Jesus and his followers. At first, these believers lived with their own families. During the third century, some believers withdrew from society to live alone and dedicate themselves to prayer. Religious hermits called anchorites lived in the desert outside Alexandria, an Egyptian city on the Nile River. The anchorites were visited by other believers who traveled to Egypt from as far away as Italy. The anchorites earned their living by making and selling baskets and mats woven from a tough grass called rush.

The first whole communities of believers were organized by the cenobites. The term *cenobite* comes from two Greek words meaning "living together." Unlike the anchorites, who lived alone, the first cenobites lived in small settlements of huts built closely together. The cenobites took their meals together, usually outdoors. Around 318, a man named Pachomius founded a cenobite community in the Egyptian desert. Pachomius wrote a set of rules for the members of his community to follow. This was the beginning of true monasticism. Under the rules of Pachomius, monks lived under the authority of an elected superior called an abbot. Each monk swore an oath of obedience to the abbot. By the time of Pachomius's death, the order had about three thousand monks living in nine separate communities, all under the rule of a single abbot. Although

Pachomius had many followers, these monasteries were not formally connected with the church, and many church leaders were suspicious of the monks.

While more and more Egyptian monasteries were founded according to the rules of Pachomius, a different type of monasticism was developing in Syria. Syrian monks lived very strict lives. Many of these monks physically punished themselves for the sins of all humanity. Some of them, called stylites, lived for years on top of tall stone pillars, going for days at a time without food or water.

A distinctive characteristic of eastern monasticism was the stylite. As penance (punishment for sins), stylites spent long periods of time on top of a pillar. On this silver casket, the stylite is surrounded by snakes, representing temptation.

Monks rejected the material world and vowed to live lives of poverty. They were often critical of the society around them, and they did not believe that the Roman Empire had been sincere in converting to Christianity. The monks felt that Christians could be divided into two groups. The *sancti,* meaning "saints," dedicated their whole lives to God. The *saeculares* were Christians in the day-to-day world who were involved in "trivial" activities. The *sancti* —that is, the monks—considered themselves the only true believers.

In time, all kinds of monastic life spread throughout Europe. Some monks traveled from place to place, while other monks lived by themselves and prayed all day long. After the rules written by Pachomius were translated into Latin, many European monasteries were founded according to Pachomius's rules. Other monasteries followed rules written by Basil, a bishop who had lived in what is now Turkey. All the Pachomian monasteries were governed by a single abbot. Under the rules of Basil, each monastery elected its own abbot. While European monasticism was at first influenced by the writings of eastern monasticism, European monks eventually produced religious works of their own. For example, in the early sixth century, the Italian monk Benedict produced a set of rules that would eventually be followed by nearly every monastery in Europe.

THE GERMANIC RULERS OF SPAIN

Roman Spain

The Iberian Peninsula (present-day Spain and Portugal) was one of the wealthiest regions of the ancient Roman Empire. Roman Iberia—called Hispania by the Romans—supplied the empire with wine, olives, grain, and metals such as gold, lead, and tin. Metals from Hispania were exported to countries as far away as India. Hispania also made important contributions to Roman culture. Three of Rome's emperors—Trajan, Hadrian, and Theodosius—were born in Hispania. Rome's most important contribution to Hispania was the Latin language. Before the Roman conquest, the peoples of Iberia spoke many different languages. The use of Latin throughout Iberia was the first step in creating a unified Iberian culture.

The Germanic Invaders

The Germanic tribes that had crossed the Rhine and invaded Gaul entered Iberia around 411 and divided up the region among the different tribes. Of these Germanic tribes, the Swabians settled in what is now northern Portugal. The Visigoths created a kingdom that covered the southern part of what is now France and extended into central Spain. In time, the Visigoths expanded their kingdom southward.

The Vandals first settled in the south of what is now Spain. The Vandals soon developed into a seafaring people and began exploring the northern coast of Africa. As the Visigoths also moved south, the Vandals lost more and more of their land in Spain. Finally, King Gaiseric led the Vandals to a new home in Africa in 429. The Vandals quickly seized large areas of Roman land in Africa. From this African kingdom, the Vandals launched attacks against both the western Roman Empire and the Byzantine Empire. In 455 the Vandals sacked Rome itself. After Justinian became the emperor of Byzantium in 527, he sent a Byzantine army into Africa to oppose the Vandals. The Byzantines destroyed the Vandal kingdom and brought northern Africa and southern Spain under Byzantine rule.

During the first half of the fifth century, the Visigoths had extended their kingdom from the Loire River in France to the southernmost tip of Iberia. Originally, the Visigoths considered their territories in France the most important part of their kingdom. However, after King Clovis of the Franks (another Germanic people) defeated the Visigoth army at the battle of Vouille in 507, the Visigoths lost all their holdings in France except for a narrow strip of land along the Mediterranean. Gradually, the Visigoths began to see themselves as an Iberian kingdom. Around 540 King Leovield moved the Visigoth capital from the French city of Toulouse to the Spanish city of Toledo.

Because the Visigoths were Arian Christians, which the church considered to be heretics, they did not mix with the Roman Christians of Iberia. Finally, King Reccared made Roman Christianity the official religion of the Visigoths in 589. The Visigoths also adopted the Latin language of their Hispanic-Roman neighbors. In 654 King Recceswinth created a set of laws for the entire Visigoth kingdom. These laws later became the basis of the law code adopted by the Spanish kingdom of Castile during the thirteenth century.

It was the Visigoth custom of electing their kings that finally brought about the collapse of the Visigoth kingdom. King Witiza, like many other Visigoth kings, hoped that after his own death his son would be elected king. However, when Witiza died in 710, the nobles and church officials who met to elect the new king rejected Witiza's son Achila. Instead, they chose a noble named Roderick as their king. Achila quickly organized a rebellion against Roderick. Count Julian, the governor of Visigoth lands in what is now Morocco, supported Achila. Julian hired an army of Muslims from north Africa to help fight on the side of Achila. The army of Muslims landed in southern Spain in 711. At the battle of Guadalete, the Muslims destroyed Roderick's Visigoth army. Now that the Muslims had landed in Spain, they were unwilling to leave. A large part of Iberia was soon ruled by the Muslims. It would be almost eight hundred years before the Muslims would be driven back to Africa.

Narbonne

Vitoria

León
Astorga
Palencia
Burgos
San Pedro
de la Nave
Quintanilla de Las Viñas
Braga
San Juan
de Baños
Barcelona
Zamora
Tarragona
Segovia
Salamanca

Toledo

Santarém
Garrazar

Mérida

Cordova
Cartagena

Seville

Málaga
Faro

Cádiz

Kingdom of the Visigoths in the seventh century

Area populated by Swabians

Area originally populated by Visigoths

Area occupied by Byzantines

Church of San Juan de Baños

This bird-shaped buckle and the religious ornament at the far left represent the elaborate art of sixth- and seventh-century Spain.

Detail from the church of Quintanilla de Las Viñas

EARLY ENGLAND

Germanic Peoples

Very little is known about the early history of the Germanic peoples who settled in Britain during the mid-400s. The earliest account of the Germanic invasion of Britain was written in 540 by a Celtic monk named Gildas. The Celts were the people who were living in Britain when the Romans invaded in A.D. 43. When the Romans abandoned Britain in 410, they left behind a population of Romanized Christian Celts who called themselves Britons. Soon after the Romans left, Picts (people native to Scotland) and Scots (Celts from Ireland who had settled in Scotland) began attacking the Britons. A Germanic tribe called the Jutes aided the Britons, and later founded the kingdom of Kent in southeast Britain.

During the fifth century, other Germanic groups, including the Angles and Saxons, invaded Britain. These Germanic groups, known collectively as the English, pushed the Celtic Britons into the far western part of Britain. These Celts became the ancestors of the modern-day inhabitants of Wales and Cornwall. While the Celts were defeated in the end, they did put up a heroic fight against the invaders. Around 470, a British general named Ambrosius Aurelianus defeated the Saxons at the battle of Mount Badon. The heroic Ambrosius became the basis for the legend of King Arthur and his Knights of the Round Table.

After the Celts were subdued, the English settled into seven separate kingdoms—Mercia, Kent, Northumbria, East Anglia, Sussex (the South Saxons), Essex (the East Saxons), and Wessex (the West Saxons). The early English were often at war with each other, and the borders of these small kingdoms were constantly changing. Each English ruler gave his soldiers gifts of gold, silver, and weapons in exchange for the soldiers' loyalty. Old English poems such as *Beowulf* describe the bond between the fighting man and his leader. A soldier who survived a battle in which his leader was killed would be disgraced for life. He was expected to fight to the death for revenge. The huge treasures that the leaders used to buy such

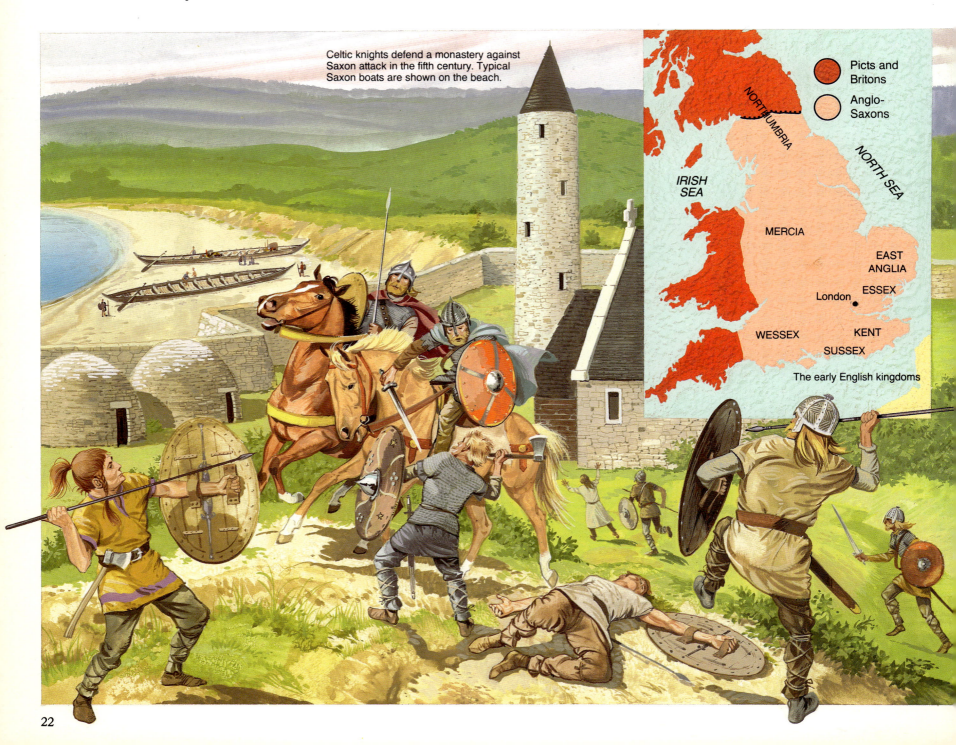

Celtic knights defend a monastery against Saxon attack in the fifth century. Typical Saxon boats are shown on the beach.

Picts and Britons

Anglo-Saxons

IRISH SEA

NORTH SEA

NORTHUMBRIA

MERCIA

EAST ANGLIA

London

ESSEX

WESSEX

KENT

SUSSEX

The early English kingdoms

loyalty have been discovered in the burial mounds of English kings.

Christianity

The slow conversion of the English to Christianity began during the sixth century. The first attempt to convert the English came from the Celts of Ireland, who had been converted to Christianity by Saint Patrick the century before. The Celtic church was isolated from mainland Europe and was independent of the pope's authority. In the mid-500s, an Irish monk named Columba built a monastery on the island of Iona off the western coast of Scotland. Monks from Iona made visits to England but had little success converting the English. In 597 Pope Gregory I sent a group of monks led by Augustine to the kingdom of Kent. King Aethelbert of Kent was the first English ruler to accept Christianity. By the time of Augustine's death in 605, the kingdoms of Kent, Essex, and East Anglia had all been converted.

In 625 King Edwin of Northumbria married Aethelberga, the daughter of King Aethelbert of Kent. By 627 Edwin had adopted the Christian faith of his wife. In 632 Edwin was murdered by Northumbrians who did not want to give up their old gods. However, the next two kings of Northumbria, Oswald and Osway, were brothers who had lived on the island of Iona. When Oswald became king, he invited monks from Iona to help convert Northumbria. Because the Celtic Christians were not under the pope's authority, the Irish monks were often in conflict with the monks sent by the pope, but in 664 the English kings agreed at the Council of Whitby that the English church should be under the rule of the pope.

Viking Rule in England

In the early 800s, Vikings from Denmark invaded England, and by the mid-800s, they had succeeded in conquering almost half of the English lands. King Alfred of Wessex saved the rest of England from conquest. After Alfred died, territorial wars continued, and Alfred's son Edward succeeded in winning back much of the Danish-ruled land, called Danelaw. It was not until 927 that Athelstan, Alfred's grandson, succeeded in becoming the first king to have direct rule over all of England. However, about a hundred years later, in 1013, the Danish regained control of England. Canute, the brother of the king of Denmark, became king of England. About fifty years later, in 1066, William the Conqueror, from an area of northern France called Normandy, invaded and conquered England.

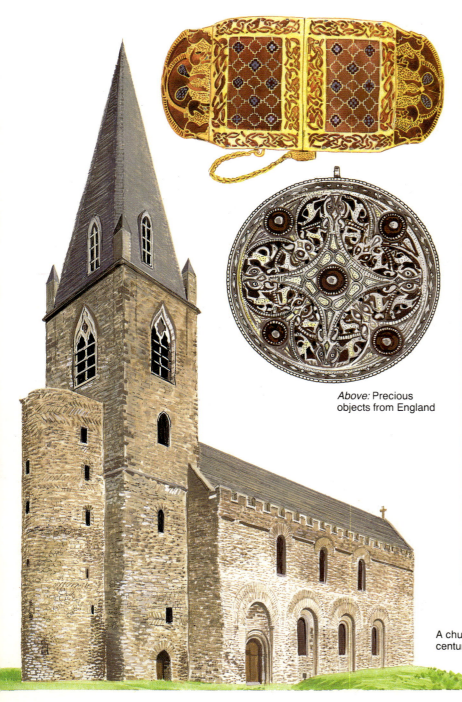

Above: Precious objects from England

A church of the eighth century

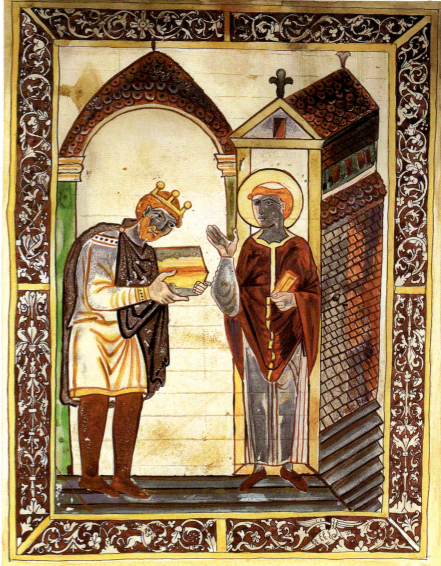

An early English king, at left, is shown holding the writings of the Venerable Bede, an English scholar of the 700s.

23

FRANKS AND LOMBARDS

The Franks

The Franks originally came from the northern area of present-day West Germany. They first moved into Roman Gaul as allies of the western Romans. The Frankish King Meroveus sent his soldiers to help the Romans fight Attila when the Huns invaded Gaul in 451. Meroveus's son Childeric later aided the western Romans against the Visigoths. As other Germanic groups were weakened by constant struggles with the Roman Empire, the Franks became the strongest of the Germanic peoples. After Childeric's fifteen-year-old son Clovis became the Frankish king in 494, the Franks began attacking the Roman settlements along the Somme and Loire rivers (both located in what is now France). As the Franks occupied more and more land, they began farming the abandoned Roman estates. Some of these estates were given to Frankish soldiers as a reward for loyalty to their king.

On Christmas Day, 496, Clovis and three thousand of his soldiers were baptized as Christians. As such, Clovis received support from the church for his wars against neighboring Germanic groups, many of whom were Arians. In 507 Clovis defeated the Arian Visigoths in Aquitaine (southern Gaul). The Visigoths eventually gave up all claims to Aquitaine and settled down to rule their lands in Spain.

The Lombards

The Lombards were a Germanic people from the northern part of present-day East Germany near the Baltic Sea. Around the year 500, the

Frankish soldiers on horseback in a rural village. In the Celtic and Roman world, great importance was given to land ownership. The Franks adopted this idea. As a result, the economy of areas under Frankish rule became primarily rural, and cities lost their importance.

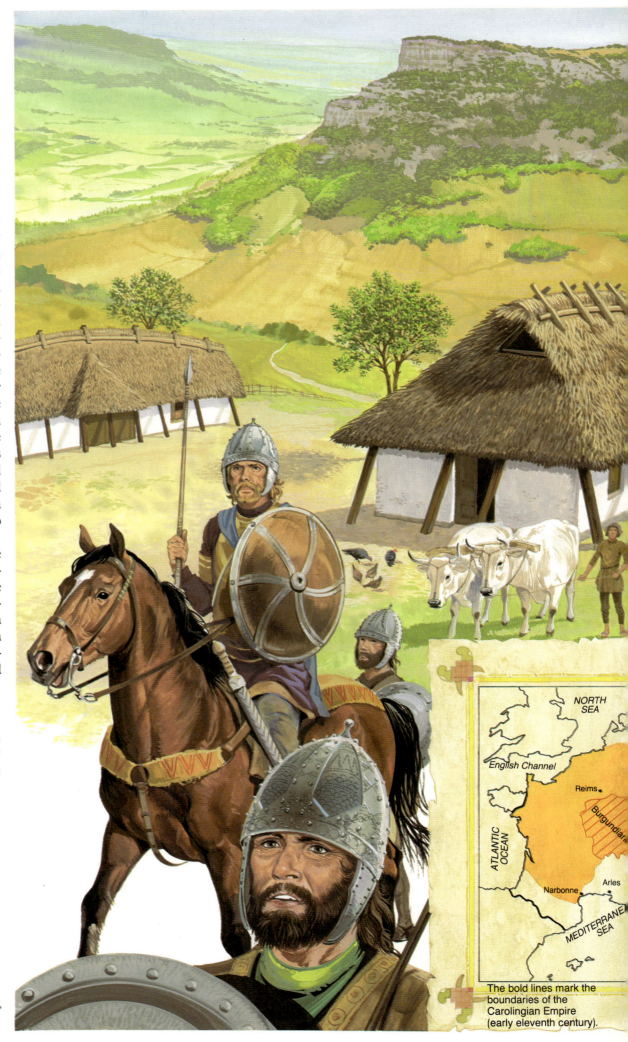

The bold lines mark the boundaries of the Carolingian Empire (early eleventh century).

Ceramics of the sixth century

Gilded bronze S-shaped buckle for women's clothes

Left:
A panel from an altar

A monastery tower

Bronze plate portraying a Lombard warrior

Saxons
Franks
Alemanni
Bavarians
Lombards

(6th, 7th, 8th centuries)

Ravenna

ADRIATIC SEA

TYRRHENIAN SEA

Rome

Benevento

Lombards moved south into what is now Hungary. While in Hungary, the Lombards adopted Arian Christianity. In the mid-500s, the Lombards formed an alliance with the Avars, a nomadic tribe from central Asia that had settled in Hungary. The Avars and Lombards together conquered a neighboring tribe called the Gepids. When the Gepids were defeated, the Lombard leader married a Gepid princess, and the Gepid people intermingled with the Lombards. The Lombards crossed the Alps into northern Italy in 568. The Byzantines had captured Italy from the Ostrogoths only a few years earlier. The Lombards seized land near what is now Venice and began a thirty-year war against the Byzantines. Gradually, the Lombards absorbed all of Byzantium's northern Italian territories except Ravenna.

When the Lombards arrived in Italy, they were divided into family groups, each led by a duke. However, under the pressure of war with Byzantium, the Lombards slowly united under a single king. Each Lombard king was chosen by election. Sometimes the Lombards elected kings from the same family. For example, six kings in a row were chosen from the Lething family. Many Lombards opposed this practice, however. King Rothari, who became the Lombard ruler in 643, forbade his own descendants to rule the Lombards for eleven generations. Rothari was also the king who gave the Lombards their code of laws. These laws, called Rothari's Edict, combined ideas from Roman law with Lombard tribal customs. Later Lombard rulers added laws of their own to Rothari's code.

The Benedictine code described every single action of monastic life in detail. Lunch had to take place in absolute silence, and the monks had to handle silverware without any noise. The meal consisted of oat or barley soup, followed by a plate of vegetables and cheese.

MONASTICISM IN EUROPE

Early Christianity in Europe

During the early Middle Ages, the spread of Christianity in Europe was resisted in many rural areas. People living in the countryside did not want to give up their local gods. When Christianity did spread, it spread to different regions in different ways. Even the forms of public worship varied from place to place. Some of the forms of Christianity that people adopted were heresies—beliefs that contradicted the teaching of the Roman church.

The Franks became the first Roman Christians among the Germanic peoples. The Visigoths in Spain and the Lombards in northern Italy were believers in Arian Christianity, which the church considered a heresy. Peoples in eastern and far northern Europe were pagans who worshiped the forces of nature. The church worked hard to convert these different groups to a single belief.

The Rule of Saint Benedict

The conversion of new peoples to Roman Christianity was due mostly to the efforts of Benedictine monks. Between 535 and 540, the Italian monk Benedict of Nursia wrote a code of behavior for monks. This code, known as *The Rule of St. Benedict,* was adopted first by Monte Cassino, a monastery in southern Italy that had been founded by Benedict in 520. According to the code, the monastic community's motto was *ora et labora,* which meant "prayer and work" in Latin. The monastery was headed by the abbot, a spiritual leader who was elected for life and to whom the monks vowed obedience. The monks prayed, read and copied religious books, and performed the manual labor that provided a livelihood for the monastery. The purpose of the code was to help the monks find God through humility and obedience. Monks were not allowed to leave the monastery. While some of the monks were ordained priests, most of the monks were ordinary people who wanted to live religious lives.

Benedict himself died in 547, and the monastery at Monte Cassino was sacked by the Lombards in 581. However, Benedict's ideas were spread by Pope Gregory I, whose book *Dialogues* contained an account of Benedict's life. Many of the monks of Monte Cassino settled in Rome in the years after the sack of their monastery. Gregory gave these monks authority to found new monasteries that followed Benedict's rule.

Gregory the Great

During the rule of Pope Gregory I, Christianity began to spread among the pagan peoples of eastern and far northern Europe. Gregory, called Gregory the Great, was born into a wealthy Roman family. When Gregory was

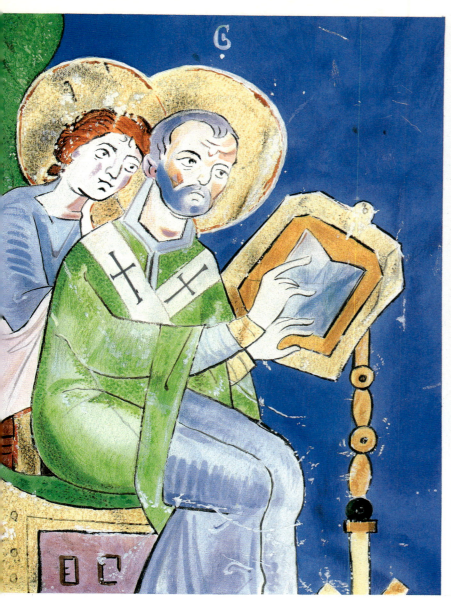

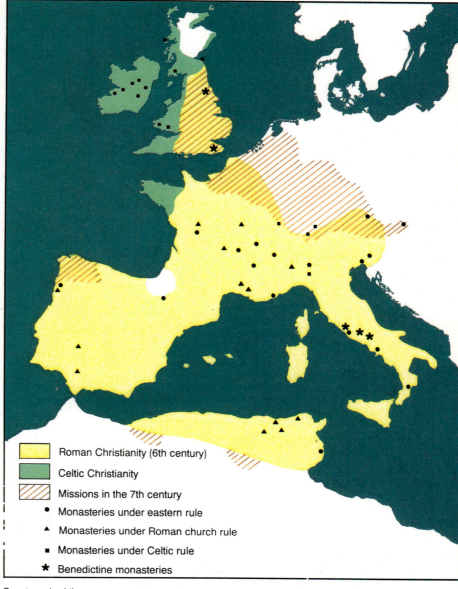

Roman Christianity (6th century)

Celtic Christianity

Missions in the 7th century

● Monasteries under eastern rule

▲ Monasteries under Roman church rule

■ Monasteries under Celtic rule

✳ Benedictine monasteries

about thirty years old, he became a monk and built seven monasteries on his family estates. In 590 Gregory became the first monk to be elected pope. As pope, Gregory used monks to convert new peoples to Christianity.

Pope Gregory sent the monk Augustine to England in 597. Aethelbert, ruler of the English kingdom of Kent, converted to Christianity. Aethelbert allowed Augustine and his followers to settle in the city of Canterbury. During the seventh century, monks from England traveled to convert the Frisians and other Germanic peoples living along the coast of the Baltic Sea. These were the same areas from which the Germanic ancestors of the English had come.

In Italy, Pope Gregory—caught between the Lombards in northern Italy and the Byzantines in southern Italy—tried to convert the Arian Lombards to Roman Christianity. Gregory's efforts were supported by Queen Theodolinda of the Lombards. While Theodolinda built many churches and monasteries, the Lombard people did not fully accept the Roman faith until the late 600s.

The papacy of Gregory the Great marked the beginning of Christianity's spread among Germanic and Slavic peoples. Gregory was the first monk elected pope, and he gave monks the mission of Christianizing new peoples.

Right: An iconoclast scraping out a portrait of Christ

Iconoclasm

In 717 Muslim armies who followed the Islamic faith tried to capture Constantinople. After the Byzantines twice defeated the attacking Muslims, the Muslims were turned away from the city. Although the Muslims themselves failed to conquer Byzantium, ideas from Islam were adopted by some Byzantines. For example, Byzantine Emperor Leo III adopted the Muslim belief that it is wrong to make a picture or statue of God. In 723 Leo ordered the destruction of all sacred images, called *icons,* in all of the Byzantine territories. The destruction of religious images was called *iconoclasm,* which means "image-breaking" in Greek. Leo's order was opposed by the pope and both the eastern monks and the Byzantines living in southern Italy. Although the order was finally taken back in 843, the dispute it caused between Constantinople and Rome pulled the Christians of the east and the west even farther apart from each other.

THE ISLAMIC EXPANSION

Arabia

The Arabian Peninsula, the birthplace of the religion called Islam, was mostly an isolated land during the seventh century. It was covered almost completely with desert. Nomads called Bedouins traveled across this desert, grazing their herds of sheep, goats, and horses on whatever small areas of grassland they could find. Each Bedouin tribe had its own area. However, if a year of extra hot weather killed the grasslands in one tribe's area, that tribe would have to fight its neighbors for new land and water.

Life along the coast of Arabia was very different from the Bedouins' life in the interior. Cities such as Mecca and Medina were important as centers of commerce between the nomadic desert tribes and sea traders from other lands.

Muhammad

Muhammad was the founder of the religion of Islam. Muhammad was born in 570 in Mecca, a city in which the Kaaba—an important religious shrine—was located. Although Muhammad married into one of the wealthiest merchant families in Mecca, he became more interested in religion than trade. When Muhammad was nearly forty, he had a series of religious visions. He believed that he had been chosen as God's messenger. Muhammad believed that there was only one God—the same God worshiped by Christians and Jews—and that every person had to submit to God's will. The name of Muhammad's religion—*Islam*—means "submission to the will of God" in Arabic. Muhammad believed that God (*Allah* in Arabic) wanted Muhammad to preach God's message. Allah's revelations are contained in Islam's sacred book, the *Koran*.

CALIPHATE OF CORDOVA

MAGHREB

IFRIQIYA

EGYPT

The military strategy used by the Arabs, who attacked Persian and Byzantine armies in prolonged raids, was a new development in the art of war.

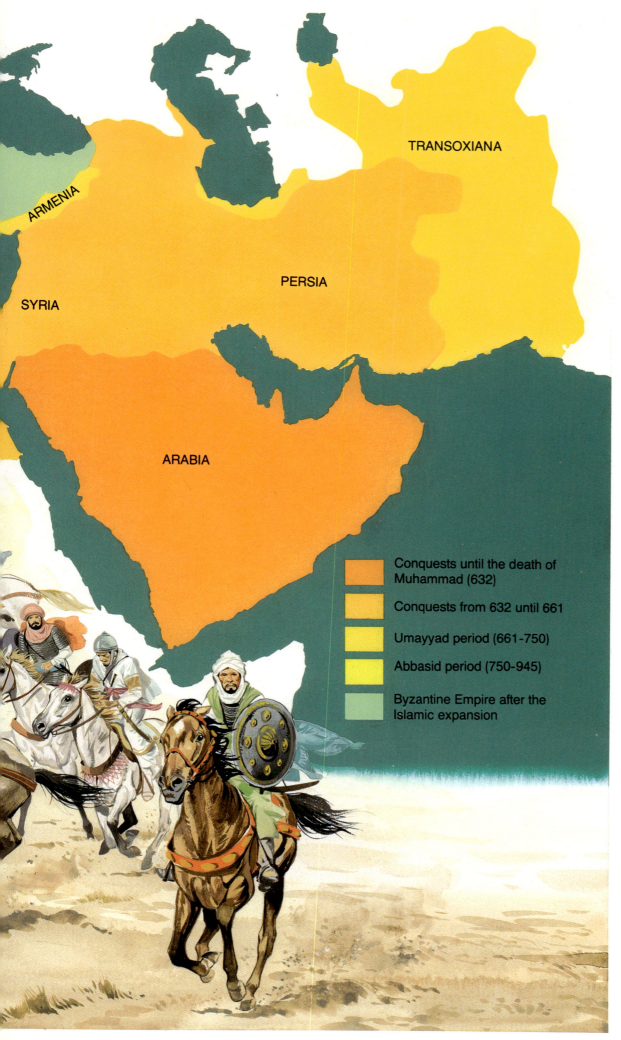

The Arabs changed the political geography of the Mediterranean, of Persia, and of the Indus River valley. The Islamic expansion reduced the Byzantine Empire and held the west in check for a long time.

TRANSOXIANA

ARMENIA

PERSIA

SYRIA

ARABIA

Conquests until the death of Muhammad (632)

Conquests from 632 until 661

Umayyad period (661-750)

Abbasid period (750-945)

Byzantine Empire after the Islamic expansion

Many people in Mecca were hostile to Muhammad's teachings. Muhammad and his followers, called Muslims, began to look around for a new home. In 622, people in the city of Medina invited Muhammad and his followers to live there. In Medina, Muhammad became both a political and a religious leader. The Hegira—Muhammad's journey to Medina—marks the beginning of official Muslim history. From Medina, Muhammad led a war to convert Mecca and the rest of Arabia to Islam. In 630, after all of Arabia was converted to Islam, Muhammad returned to Mecca. He died there in 632.

Expansion in the Umayyad Period

After Muhammad's death, his followers chose a caliph ("successor" in Arabic) to lead the Islamic community. The first caliph was Abu Bakr, one of Muhammad's earliest followers. After only two years of rule, Abu Bakr died in 634. The next caliph, Omar, expanded Muslim rule beyond Arabia. Syria, Egypt, and Persia (present-day Iran) soon accepted the religion and leadership of the Muslim caliph. When Omar was murdered in 644, he was succeeded by Otham, the leader of the Umayyad family. The Umayyads fought for power against the followers of Ali, the cousin and son-in-law of Muhammad. When Ali was murdered in 661, the Umayyads took full control of the Muslim empire. When Muawiya, the Umayyad governor of Syria, became caliph in 661, he moved the empire's capital to the Syrian city of Damascus. For ninety years, the Umayyads ruled an empire that eventually extended from India to Spain. Although the empire included many different peoples, only Arabs were allowed to hold offices in the government. The discontent of the non-Arab Muslims would eventually cause the overthrow of the Umayyad rulers.

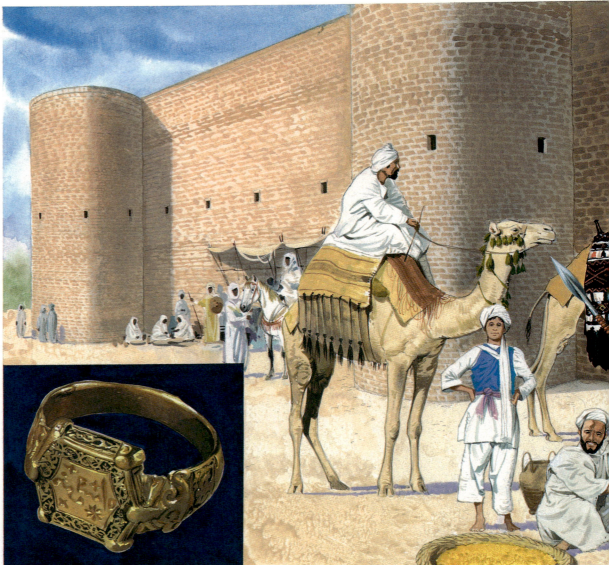

Golden ring, Iran (tenth-eleventh centuries)

A detail of the Mosque of Bib-Mardum (tenth century) in Spain. A mosque is a Muslim place of worship.

ISLAM DURING THE ABBASID AGE

Sunnites and Shiites

During the years after Muhammad's death, Muslims became divided. Two groups, the Sunnites and the Shiites, disagreed over the issue of who should succeed Muhammad as the leader of Islam.

The Sunnites believed that the caliph's rule could be kept faithful to Muhammad's teachings by following the Sunna. The Sunna was an explanation of the Koran that also included ideas from the traditions of the Islamic community.

The Shiites believed that only a descendant of Muhammad should be the leader of Islam. Because the Umayyad caliph was not a relative of Muhammad, the Shiites did not recognize his authority. The Shiites believed that Ali, the cousin and son-in-law of Muhammad, was the rightful leader of Islam. Ali was murdered in 661. Although the last of Ali's direct descendants died in 873, the split between Sunnites and Shiites continues even today. About 80 percent of the Muslims in the world today are Sunnites. Iran is the only country in the world that is mostly Shiite.

The Abbasids

The Abbasids took power from the Umayyads in the middle of the eighth century. The Abbasids were led by Abu al Abbas, a descendant of Muhammad. Most of Abu al Abbas's followers were Persians and Arabs living in the area that is present-day Iran. These people had not liked being ruled by an Umayyad authority in far-off Damascus. After the Abbasid victory over the Umayyads, the capital was moved to Baghdad, a city in what is now Iraq. The Abbasid caliph was assisted by the vizier, his chief adviser. The vizier managed a large group of secretaries, treasury officials, and military leaders. These government officials worked both in Baghdad and in the distant territories of the empire. Under the Abbasids, Islam became a true blend of many cultures. Although Arabic remained the written language, ideas from the older Persian civilization and from the Greek books collected in Baghdad's libraries produced a rich new civilization that is often called the golden age of Islam.

Around the beginning of the ninth century, areas at the edges of the empire split off into independent Muslim states. By the mid-800s, Baghdad ruled only the central part of the

Mosques were not exclusively religious meeting places. In fact, markets arose around their walls.

empire—an area consisting of Armenia and Syria as they are shown on the map on pages 28-29.

Islam in Spain

After Muslims from northern Africa defeated the Visigoths in Spain, the Muslim army had moved north toward central Europe. Charles Martel halted this advance in 732, when his Frankish army defeated the Muslims at Poitiers, a city in what is now France. Afterwards, the Muslims settled in Spain. Many Spanish Christians converted to Islam, and those who wanted to keep the Christian religion had to pay a special tax. The bishop of Toledo ruled over the Christians in the Muslim-ruled areas.

The Muslims of Spain supported the Umayyads against the Abbasids. In 756 the last surviving member of the Umayyad family fled from Damascus to Spain. He established a new Umayyad caliphate (office) at the Spanish city of Cordova. The Cordovan caliphate lasted until 1013, when rival Muslims overthrew the caliph.

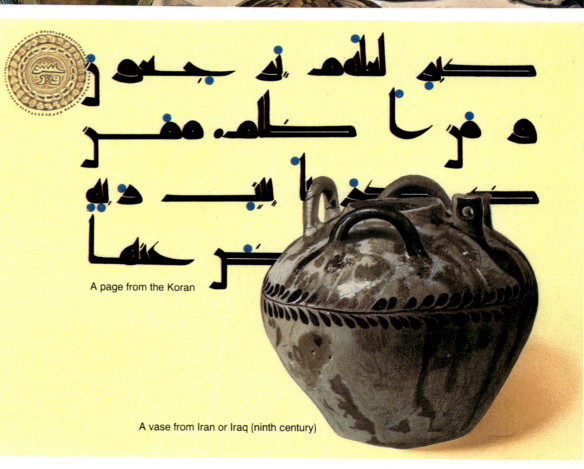

A page from the Koran

A vase from Iran or Iraq (ninth century)

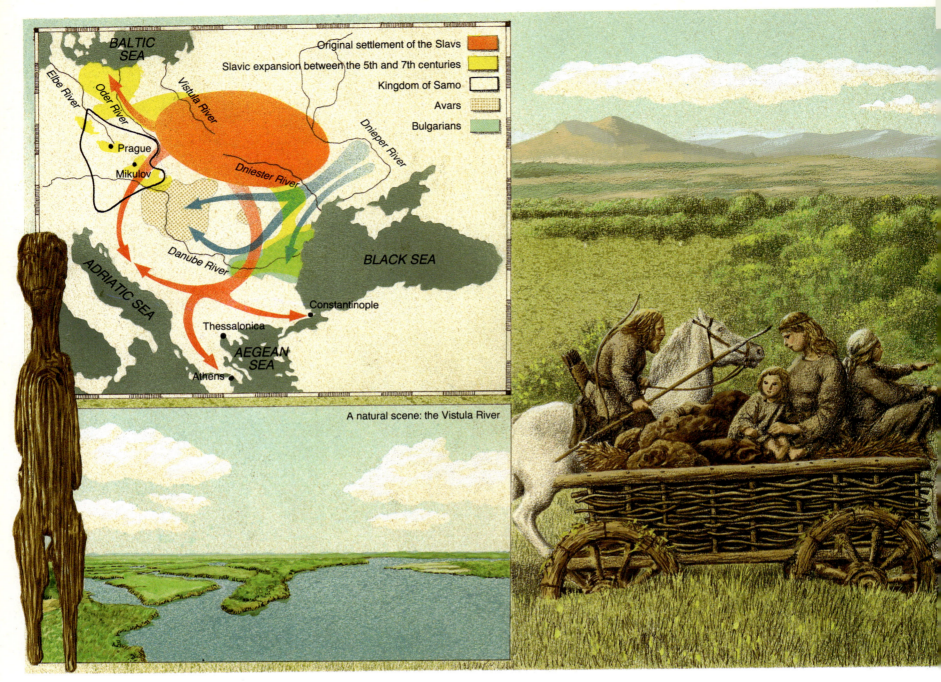

Original settlement of the Slavs

Slavic expansion between the 5th and 7th centuries

Kingdom of Samo

Avars

Bulgarians

BALTIC SEA

Elbe River

Oder River

Vistula River

Dnieper River

Prague

Mikulov

Dniester River

ADRIATIC SEA

Danube River

BLACK SEA

Constantinople

Thessalonica

AEGEAN SEA

Athens

A natural scene: the Vistula River

A wooden statue representing the worship of fertility (sixth century)

THE SLAVS

The Slavic Peoples

The Slavs originally came from the area of the Pripet marshes, a region that lies between the Dnieper and the Vistula rivers. From this location, the Slavs spread outward to occupy the central part of what later became Russia. Eventually, the Slavs moved into every part of eastern Europe, from the Baltic Sea in the north to the Balkan peninsula in the south.

From their earliest history, the Slavs were an agricultural people. They grew grains such as barley, millet, rye, and oats. Other crops such as beets, onions, and garlic were also grown. The Slavs even produced hemp and flax, plants whose tough fibers are used to make cloth. They also kept animals such as pigs, goats, and oxen. Like the early Germanic peoples, the Slavs were agricultural nomads. When the soil they farmed was too worn out to produce any more crops, they moved on and started farming in a new spot.

The earliest Slavic houses were cabins made of timber and were partly submerged in the earth. A village might consist of a dozen such houses arranged in the shape of a horseshoe around a central space that served as a meeting area. All the people in a village were members of the same family. The chief of the village was either the oldest member of the family or a person chosen by election. Sometimes the widow of a leader who died would take her husband's place as the head of a family group.

All the members of a village owned their

A Slavic village

A wooden Slavic house. The roof is made of straw; inside, there is a fireplace.

A lead statue representing a horse

The Slavs moved with the women, children, and goods on wagons pulled by oxen and guided by men armed with bows and arrows.

goods in common. The woodlands surrounding the village were also considered common property. In the woods, the Slavs caught fur-bearing animals such as ermine and squirrel. These furs were the earliest products the Slavs traded with neighboring peoples.

The early Slavs were pagans and worshiped a large number of gods. The most important Slavic gods were the sun god Svarog and the thunder god Perun. During the 800s, many Slavs converted to Christianity.

The Migrations

Sometime between the third and fifth centuries, the Slavs began moving from their original location. The historian of the Ostrogoths, Jordanes, reports that the Slavs had settled in the area of the Danube River by 551. No one is really sure why the Slavs migrated. Unlike the Germanic peoples, who all left one place and moved to another, some Slavs remained in their old territories while others moved into new areas. As the Slavs were scattered over a wider

and wider area, the culture and language of each group of Slavs became very different from those of the others. After the time of the migrations, the story of the Slavs is really the story of three separate peoples—the west Slavs, the south Slavs, and the east Slavs. The west Slavs settled around the Danube River. The south Slavs moved into the Balkan peninsula. The east Slavs remained in the area of the Pripet marshes and became the ancestors of today's Polish and Russian peoples.

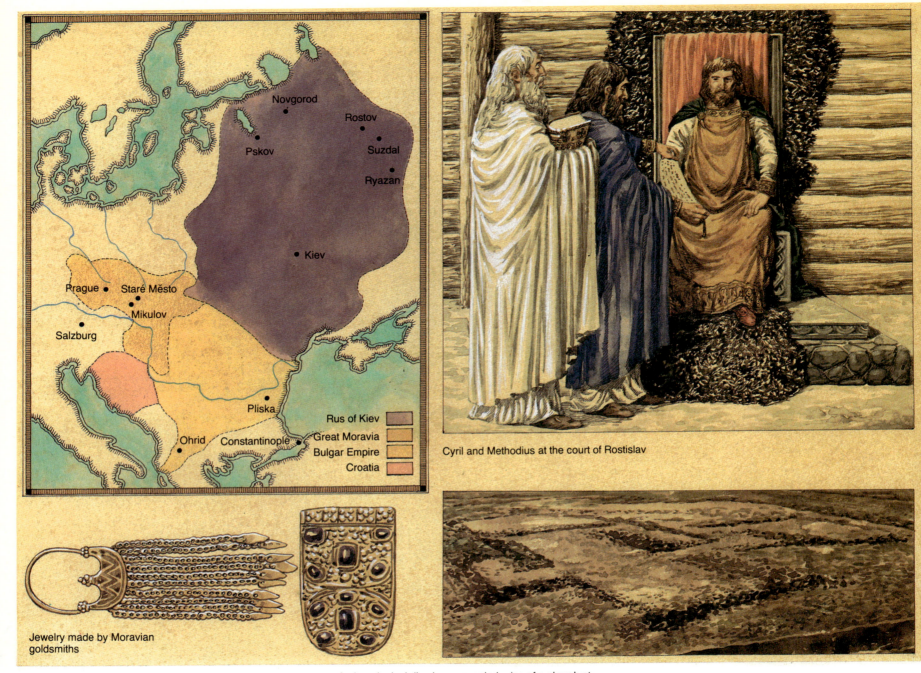

Cyril and Methodius at the court of Rostislav

Jewelry made by Moravian goldsmiths

Archaeological digs have revealed ruins of a church at Staré Město, near Prague in Czechoslovakia. It is thought to be a monastery.

THE SLAVIC KINGDOMS

The West Slavs

The Slavs who settled around the Danube River lived under the rule of the Avars, a people from central Asia. During the early 600s, a Slavic leader named Samo organized the Slavs into a union to oppose the Avars. For a short time, these Slavs lived under Samo as an independent kingdom. However, after Samo died in 658, the Avars once again subdued the Slavs. In the early 800s, the Frankish Emperor Charlemagne destroyed the Avar kingdom. The Slavs who had aided Charlemagne were given land in the western part of what is now Czechoslovakia. In 818 this area became a single kingdom under the rule of King Mojmir. This kingdom was known as Great Moravia. Over the next eighty years, Great Moravia expanded to include all of Czechoslovakia, the southern part of today's Poland, and the western part of what is now Hungary.

In 863 the Moravian ruler Rostislav invited two Greek monks named Cyril and Methodius to bring Christianity to Moravia. Cyril translated the Gospels into Slavonic. At this time, the Slavs did not have a written language. Cyril gave the Slavs an alphabet of his own invention called Glagolitic. The Moravian church, under the leadership of Methodius, was independent of both Constantinople and Rome. Moravian priests performed the Mass in Slavonic.

In 869 Rostislav was captured and blinded by enemies. Svatopluk became the new ruler of Moravia. Svatopluk wanted the Moravian church to join the Roman church headed by the pope. After the death of Methodius, Svatopluk forbade Moravian priests to perform the Mass in Slavonic, and Latin replaced Slavonic as the language of worship in the Moravian church. Pope Stephen V accepted Moravia into the church of Rome around the year 888.

Svatopluk died in 894. His sons fought each other for the crown of Moravia. A weakened Moravia was easily conquered by the Hungarians in 907.

The South Slavs

According to the Byzantine historian Procopius, the Slavs first arrived in the Balkans north of Greece during the early 520s. Together with

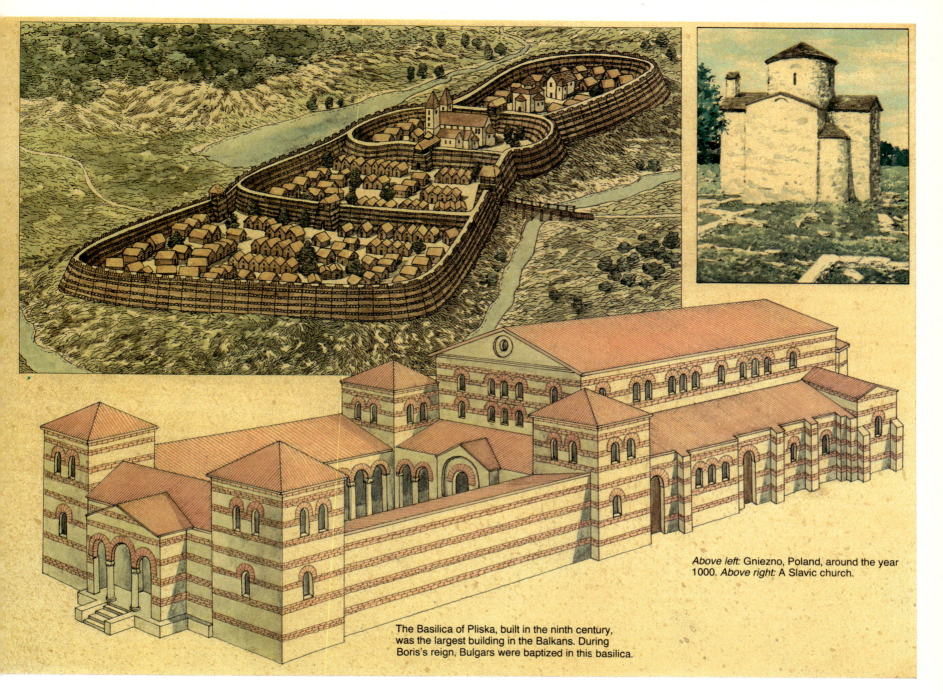

Above left: Gniezno, Poland, around the year 1000. *Above right:* A Slavic church.

The Basilica of Pliska, built in the ninth century, was the largest building in the Balkans. During Boris's reign, Bulgars were baptized in this basilica.

the Avars, the Slavs began attacking Greece in the 580s. In about 670, a Turkic people called the Bulgars invaded the eastern part of the Balkans. The Bulgars pushed the Avars out of the area. The Slavs who lived in the western part of the Balkans later formed the kingdom of Croatia. The Slavs who remained in the eastern Balkans lived side by side with the Bulgars. Bulgars and Slavs intermarried. The Bulgars adopted the language of the Slavs, and the two groups merged into a single people. Although this new people was actually a blend of Bulgars and Slavs, the term *Bulgar* came to be used for all the members of this group. The kingdom founded by this people became known as Bulgaria. Bulgaria soon expanded southward into Greece and westward into what is now Yugoslavia. In 865, under King Boris I, the Bulgars were converted to Christianity. Like the early Moravian church, the Bulgarian church was independent of both the Roman and the Byzantine churches.

Shortly after Boris died in 889, the area around the Danube River was invaded by the Hungarians. The Hungarian presence cut off all contact between the south Slavs and the west Slavs. The Slavic languages spoken by the Bulgars became very different from those of the west Slavs. During the eleventh century, Bulgarian translators began using an alphabet called Cyrillic. This alphabet, which had been invented by the Greek monk Cyril, was based on Greek letters. The Cyrillic alphabet gradually replaced Glagolitic writing. Today, the Cyrillic alphabet is still used to write the Russian, Serbian, and Bulgarian languages.

The East Slavs

During the eighth and ninth centuries, the Slavs who lived along the rivers of Russia were ruled by groups of seafarers from Scandinavia. These Scandinavians, who were later called Vikings, were first called *Rus,* meaning "rowers." The land they ruled became known as Russia. According to the earliest written history of Russia, the Slavs who lived along the Volkhov River had driven the Vikings out of their land by the mid-800s. However, after these Slavs began to fight among themselves, they invited the Vikings back to restore order. The Viking leader Rurik arrived in the city of Novgorod in 862. From Novgorod, which was located on the Volkhov River, Rurik ruled over an area that became the first Russian kingdom. Oleg, Rurik's successor, moved the capital from Novgorod to the city of Kiev on the Dnieper River. The princes of Kiev remained the rulers of Russia until the 1200s.

THE ECONOMY

Agriculture

During the fifth century, Germanic farmers moved onto the large estates abandoned by the Romans. The Germanic peoples brought with them farming methods very different from those of the Romans. Roman farmers, who used a lightweight plow, could farm hillsides and oddly shaped fields. The Germanic farmers used a much heavier plow that rolled on wheels and was pulled by oxen. Because it was much harder to turn the heavy plow, the Germanic farmers plowed their fields in long, straight rows and could only farm on flat land.

Germanic farmers owned their fields in common and worked together on them. Each Germanic settlement had two large fields. Each year one field was planted with grain crops, such as rye and oats, while the second field was left unplanted. Sheep and oxen grazed on the unplanted field, and their droppings fertilized the soil. The following year, the field in which the animals had grazed was planted with crops. The field that had been planted the previous year was then used to graze the animals.

Much of northern Europe was made up of forests and swamps. While these thick forests limited the amount of land that could be farmed, the forests themselves were a valuable resource. The Germanic peoples hunted deer and other animals that lived in the forest. From the forest the Germanic farmers gathered the wood they burned to heat their homes and collected acorns to feed their pigs.

The piece of farmland held by a group of farmers was called a mark. Under Germanic tribal law, the farmers who shared a mark could forbid outsiders from settling on their land. However, during the eighth and ninth centuries, Germanic kings began to give ownership of the marks to high-ranking soldiers and church officials. The farmers who lived on the mark were placed under the authority of the new landowner. These landowners would become the most powerful social class of the Middle Ages.

Trade

For a long time, the Germanic economy—based on hunting and primitive farming—only produced enough to supply the most basic needs. Then, during the first century A.D., Germanic soldiers received payments of silver for serving in the Roman army. With this silver they bought goods from the Roman merchants who had settled along the Rhine River. These merchants sold wine and small articles such as cooking utensils. The German word for a business person—*kaufmann*—comes from *caupo*, the Latin term for a small merchant.

During the fifth century, as the Roman administrative structure collapsed, the old Roman roads fell into disrepair. Farmers tore up the paving stones to build stone houses and repair their stone fences. Rivers became the new highways of Europe. The Rhine and Moselle rivers in Germany, long important as trade routes between Roman Gaul and the Germanic areas outside the empire, now tied together the Germanic kingdoms of western and central Europe.

The picture shows a Germanic village, with the ruins of a Roman villa (country estate home) in the background.

A capital of the tenth century, with Arabic inscriptions. A capital consists of the top part of a column and the base of the architectural structure, such as the arch, supported by the column itself. The capital's decorations distinguished the column from the supported structure.

To the early Germanic peoples, art mostly served a decorative purpose, as shown by their beautiful swords, shields, and helmets. The combination of gold and precious gems was typical of the Germanic style.

ART OF THE EARLY MIDDLE AGES

Byzantine Art

Constantinople was built by Constantine, the first Christian Roman emperor, to be the capital of the Christian empire. Constantinople was the crossroads of trade between Europe and Asia, and the art that emerged from Byzantine artists during the fourth century was a merging of eastern and western styles. Byzantine art was characterized by realistic figures that were very lifelike, as in the classical Greek and Roman traditions. The figures were also decorated with very fanciful and abstract patterns and designs, in the eastern tradition.

Before the Christian church was established, the pagan Romans had decorated their temples with statues of their gods. Many early Christians felt that such statues were too much like the graven images forbidden by the Bible, and so statues were never very popular with the Byzantines. The art at which the Byzantines excelled was the mosaic. A mosaic is a picture made of tiny bits of such materials as glass and stone. A beautiful mosaic of Emperor Justinian and Empress Theodora decorates the interior of the church of St. Apollinare Nuova in Ravenna, Italy.

During the 500s, Justinian ordered the construction of the most splendid of all Byzantine churches—Hagia Sophia (meaning "divine wisdom") in Constantinople. Built between the years 532 and 562, Hagia Sophia became the religious center of the Byzantine empire. The huge dome is over 170 feet tall and is supported by a square base and massive columns and arches. Huge mosaics covered the walls and columns of Hagia Sophia. The inside of the church was decorated with painted wooden panels. On these panels, Byzantine artists painted icons—pictures of Christ and other religious figures such as saints and angels. These images were considered sacred and were decorated with gold and bright colors.

When Muslim Turks conquered Constantinople in 1453, they turned Hagia Sophia into a mosque for the worship of Allah (God). Because the Muslims believed it was sinful to make a picture of God, they covered the art inside the church. Hagia Sophia is still standing in modern Istanbul. It has remained a mosque to this day.

Art of the Germanic Peoples

Because the early Germanic peoples often moved from place to place, they valued only what they could carry with them on their travels—small carvings in ivory, small objects made of gold, armor, and weapons. The Germanic peoples were masters in the art of metalworking. Precious objects were decorated with geometric designs or patterns of wandering lines. Sometimes these patterns formed the bodies of birds and other animals. When the Germanic peoples became more settled and converted to Christianity, these traditional designs were used in Germanic religious art. Monks copied pages of sacred books by hand and decorated them with geometric patterns. Germanic churches were decorated with objects skillfully worked in gold and silver.

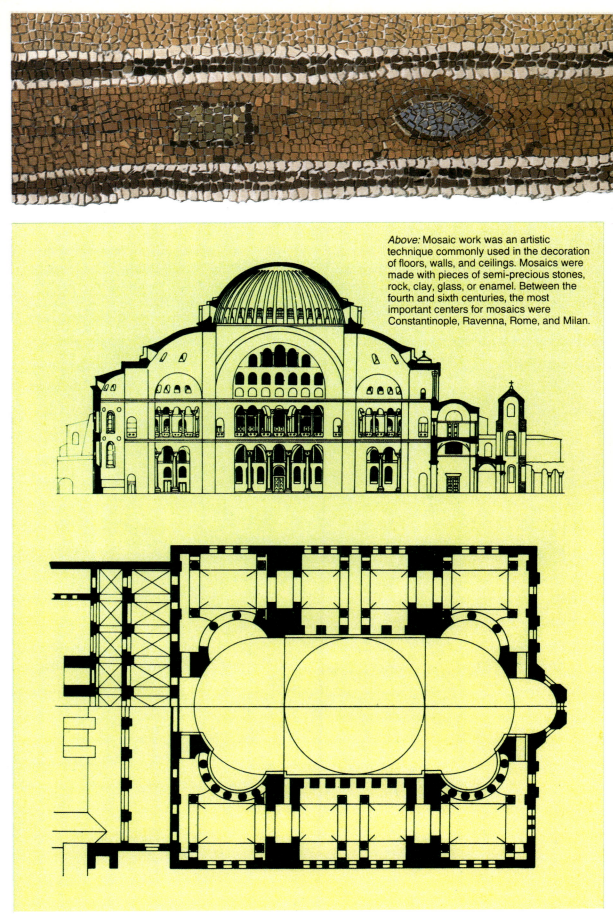

Above: Mosaic work was an artistic technique commonly used in the decoration of floors, walls, and ceilings. Mosaics were made with pieces of semi-precious stones, rock, clay, glass, or enamel. Between the fourth and sixth centuries, the most important centers for mosaics were Constantinople, Ravenna, Rome, and Milan.

Drawings of Hagia Sophia in Constantinople. Begun by Emperor Justinian, it was completed in 562. In its original version, the interior was particularly sumptuous. Decorated capitals, mosaics with golden backgrounds, gold and silver objects, and purple drapery all contributed to making the church the masterpiece of Byzantine art.

Although the Germanic peoples were not very skilled architects before the eighth century, the Ostrogoth King Theodoric built several beautiful churches and palaces in the early 500s. One of the greatest Ostrogoth buildings is the tomb of Theodoric, still standing in the Italian city of Ravenna. The roof of Theodoric's tomb is a single block of stone weighing more than 450 tons.

Art of the Celts

In England and Ireland, the Celts were converted to Christianity during the fifth and sixth centuries. The Celts also used their art to serve their religion. They built monasteries that became centers of religious art. The Celts decorated beautiful pages illustrating the Gospels. Celtic monks drew on pages of parchment, a writing surface made from very thin lamb's skin. On parchment, they created illuminated manuscripts with miniatures of animals and Biblical characters, interlaced with colorful geometric shapes and colored with gold and silver. The manuscripts were sometimes bound in leather and decorated with gold, silver, and precious stones to glorify the Gospels.

The most famous Celtic illuminated manuscript is called the *Book of Kells*. It was created in a monastery in Kells, Ireland, between the mid-700s and early 800s.

THE GERMANIC PEOPLES AND CHRISTIAN ROME

Italy After the Fall of Rome

August 23, 476, is often used as the date that marks the end of the Roman empire of the west. On that day the Germanic soldier Odoacer overthrew the last western emperor, the sixteen-year-old Romulus Augustulus. Odoacer and his followers were Germanic soldiers in the Roman army. These soldiers had helped defend Rome against other Germanic groups hostile to the empire. When economic problems left Rome unable to pay its army, the Germanic soldiers demanded land as payment for their services. Emperor Romulus Augustulus refused. Odoa-cer and his followers marched on Rome and removed Romulus Augustulus from power. Odoacer made himself the ruler of Italy and demanded that the Byzantine emperor recognize him as Byzantium's representative in the west. While Odoacer and Byzantine Emperor Zeno managed to make a brief alliance, a quarrel broke out between them over the choice of a new pope. In the late 480s, an army of Ostrogoths led by Theodoric was sent by Emperor Zeno to overthrow Odoacer. By 493 Theodoric had defeated Odoacer and was recognized by Zeno as the king of Italy and Dalmatia (a part of present-day Yugoslavia). Theodoric built his capital at Ravenna, a city on the northeast coast of Italy.

Theodoric wanted to be a ruler as great as the Roman emperors who had ruled Italy before him. He built many palaces and churches. One church—St. Apollinare Nuova—still stands in Ravenna. Ravenna also became a center of learning. During this period, Theodoric's friend and adviser, the Roman philosopher Boethius, wrote his great philosophical work.

Religious differences between the Ostrogoths and the Byzantines would destroy Theodoric's kingdom. Theodoric and many of his people were believers in the Arian heresy. When Byzan-

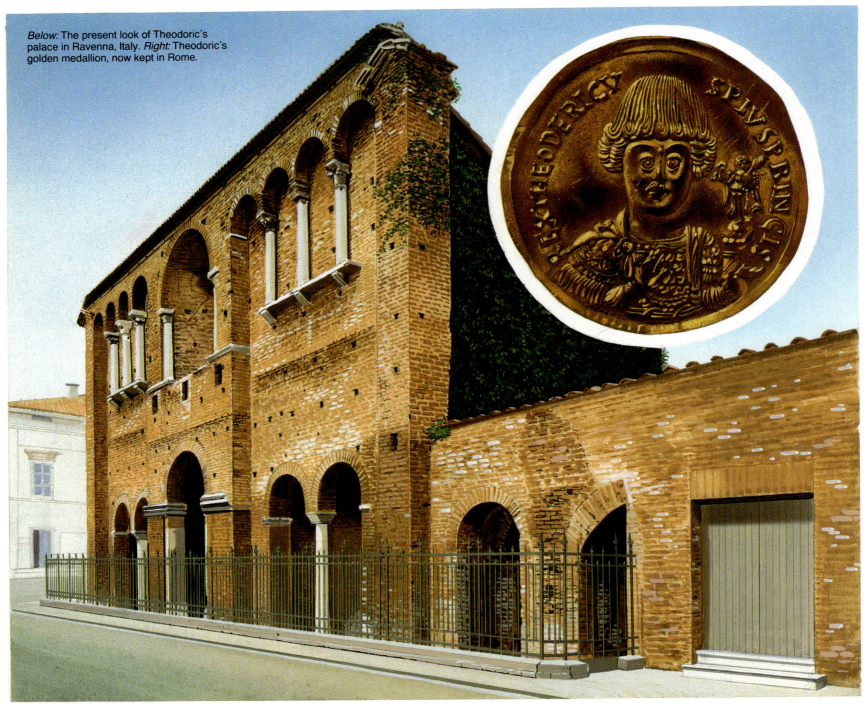

Below: The present look of Theodoric's palace in Ravenna, Italy. *Right:* Theodoric's golden medallion, now kept in Rome.

tine Emperor Justin declared that pagans, heretics, and Jews could no longer hold office in the Byzantine government, a group of Christians led by Boethius tried to overthrow Theodoric in 524. Theodoric had the rebels put to death. After Theodoric's own death, his Christian daughter Amalasuntha became the new ruler. This time, the Arians rebelled and murdered Amalsuntha in 535. Emperor Justinian, who considered Amalsuntha a representative of the Byzantine government, used this murder as an excuse to send troops to Italy. By 552 Italy was completely under Justinian's rule.

Roman Law and Germanic Law

As the Germanic kings had replaced the Romans as the rulers of western Europe, many Germanic peoples adopted the laws of Rome or used Roman and Germanic law together. The Visigoths in Spain used many ideas from Roman law in writing their law code. Like Roman law, the Visigoth code specified different punishments for the members of different social classes. One unique feature of Visigoth law was that, for certain very serious crimes such as murder, the wrongdoer would be handed over to the family of the victim for punishment.

While the Visigoths created a code of laws for their kingdom, other Germanic groups continued to live under their own tribal laws. After the western Roman empire had collapsed and Gaul was ruled by Franks, the Frankish kings used separate laws for the Romans and the Franks living in the same kingdom. Generally, Roman law demanded physical punishments, while Frankish law required wrongdoers to pay fines. For example, a Roman who committed murder would be put to death, while a Frank who committed murder would have to pay a sum of gold. Frankish law specified the exact amount to be paid for each crime.

However, the most important feature of Frankish law was that it did not allow women to own land. Because the Franks based political authority on the ownership of land, no woman could rule the Frankish kingdom. During the fourteenth century, the king of France would try to revive this ancient law to prevent the king of England from inheriting his mother's land in France.

The conversion of a Lombard soldier. The Lombards remained Arian for a long time, and their conversion to the Roman church was slow and difficult.

Two sides of a Frankish rectangular burial stone. *Above left:* A warrior grooming his hair. Long hair was a typical feature of free, armed men. *Above right:* A man with a halo holding a spear in his right hand. His feet rest on undefined figures, most likely snakes or dragons. The man is Jesus Christ, who is depicted as a warrior defeating the spirits of evil.

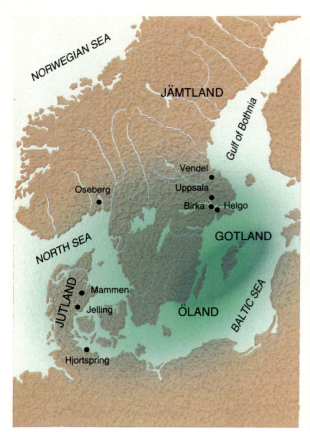

The map shows the most significant archaeological remains of early Scandinavian culture discovered thus far.

THE PEOPLES OF THE NORTH

Scandinavia

Scandinavia is the name given to the northernmost region of Europe. Scandinavia today consists of the modern nations of Norway, Sweden, Denmark, Iceland, and Finland. During the early Middle Ages, the geographic isolation of the northern areas limited the contacts between the Germanic peoples of Scandinavia and other cultures. Unlike the Germanic peoples of central Europe, many of whom adopted the Latin language and Christian religion of the Romans, the Germanic peoples of Scandinavia, also called Vikings, remained more free from outside influences. The Scandinavians continued to speak Germanic languages and to worship their old gods.

The Scandinavians lived on small farms built close to waterways. These farms produced rye, barley, oats, and cabbage. The Scandinavians also kept animals such as geese, sheep, goats, and cattle. A single large farm building made of timber and roofed with sod provided housing for as many as a dozen people, all members of the same family. A group of four or five such buildings formed a community. All of the people who lived in a community were related to each other. The community was headed by a leader called an earl. A group of communities

Some of the daily activities on a Scandinavian farm

might form a loose alliance and choose one of these earls as a king. However, there were many of these kings, and they were often at war with each other. Scandinavia was slow to unite into larger kingdoms. Around 870 Harald Fairhair became the first king to rule all of Norway. Denmark and Sweden did not become single kingdoms until the late 900s.

Culture and Religion

Scandinavian kings did not necessarily pass their authority on to their children. Kings were chosen for their abilities as leaders and warriors. Because of this, the Scandinavians were anxious to fight wars, perform heroic deeds, and conquer foreign lands. In long poems called sagas, the Scandinavians recorded the stories of bloody family feuds that lasted for generations. Scandinavian kings were proud to have nicknames such as "blood-axe."

Because the men were so often away fighting wars, it was the women who usually ran the day-to-day affairs of the community. Viking women had more rights and prestige than other European women of that time. For example, they could own their own land and other property, could share in their husbands' wealth, and could be granted divorces.

The Scandinavians were pagans who worshiped many gods. The most important god was Odin, the god of poetry, magic, and war. Another important god was Thor, the god of thunder. The Scandinavians believed that heroes who died in battle were taken after death to a great hall called Valhalla. In Valhalla the warriors fought battles for all eternity. For the Scandinavians, fighting a war was the greatest happiness. People who died peacefully were believed to spend eternity in a gloomy place called Hel.

Right: The remains of a fortified Scandinavian settlement, perhaps dating from the 400s

Below: A piece of a mold used to make helmets, showing warriors who were followers of Odin

Above: A bronze ornament of the eighth century

In this settlement, cemetery stones are laid out in the shapes of ships. This shows the importance of navigation to the Scandinavians.

Scandinavians traveled to distant lands to carry on trade.

THE CAROLINGIANS

The Franks After Clovis

When the Frankish ruler Clovis died in 511, his kingdom was divided among his four sons. Soon afterward, three of these sons also died. Lothair, the remaining son, became the ruler of the entire Frankish kingdom. When Lothair died, the kingdom was divided among Lothair's own four sons, and the Frankish kingdom again became four separate kingdoms: Neustria consisted of what is now the northwestern part of France; Austrasia consisted of the northeastern part of present-day France and much of present-day West Germany; Burgundy consisted of the southeastern part of France; and Aquitaine was in the southwestern part of France. (The map on page 46 shows the borders of these kingdoms.)

While Lothair's grandson Lothair II did manage to reunite the Frankish kingdoms for a short time in the early 600s, the kings who ruled the Franks were generally weak kings, called the Merovingian monarchs. During the reign of these kings, the chief official in each king's government began running the kingdom. These officials, who were called the mayors of the palace, were in charge of both the civil government and the army.

In 687 Pepin of Heristal, the mayor of Austrasia, defeated the mayor of Neustria in battle. Pepin became the mayor of both kingdoms. When Pepin died in 714, his two grandsons became the mayors of Austrasia and Neustria. However, these grandsons turned out to be as weak as the Merovingians themselves. A rebellion soon broke out in Neustria. Pepin's illegitimate son Charles seized control of both kingdoms. He punished the rebels and gave land and positions in the government to his supporters. Charles, who was known as Charles Martel (Charles the Hammer), was a strong leader who put new lands under his rule. Burgundy and Alemannia, a land southeast of Austrasia, became part of the area ruled by Charles. In 732 Charles defeated Muslim invaders from Spain, saving central Europe from conquest by the Muslims.

When Charles died in 741, the kingdom was divided between his two sons. Carloman became the mayor of Austrasia, while Pepin the Short became the mayor of Neustria. Six years later, Carloman gave up his kingdom to join a monastery. Pepin the Short became ruler of all the Frankish lands, though he did not have the title of king. In 751 Pepin called an assembly of Frankish leaders. This assembly elected Pepin as their new king. Childeric III, the last of the Merovingian kings, was imprisoned in a monastery. The kings descended from Pepin made up the Carolingian Dynasty.

The Donation of Pepin

In 754 Pope Stephen II traveled to Pepin's kingdom to crown Pepin king of the Franks in a religious ceremony. The pope also came to beg for Pepin's help against the Lombard rulers of northern Italy. The Lombards had gradually occupied all of the Byzantine territories in Italy, and now threatened the pope's own lands. In 755 Pepin sent a Frankish army into Italy. Pepin defeated the Lombard king and seized a large area of Lombard land in northern Italy. This land, called the Donation of Pepin, was given by Pepin to Pope Stephen II. The Donation of Pepin was the beginning of the Papal States, which were ruled by the pope until 1871.

An eighth-century goblet

The Carolingian army returns from a battle.

CHARLEMAGNE

Charles the Great

Charles the Great, known as Charlemagne, was the son of Pepin the Short. Unlike his father, Charlemagne was a very tall man—about 6 feet, 6 inches (2 meters) in height. This giant of a man would become a giant in history: he would be the most powerful ruler in the Europe of his time.

Pepin the Short died in 768, and Charlemagne became the ruler of the Franks three years later. Over the next forty-three years, Charlemagne would double the size of his kingdom and would revolutionize life in Europe in many ways.

Charlemagne began his military career with a war against the Lombards. Pope Adrian I asked for Charlemagne's help against the Lombard King Desiderius in 772. Desiderius had recaptured some of the Lombard lands in Italy that Pepin the Short had given to the pope. Charlemagne defeated Desiderius and returned to Adrian the lands taken by the Lombards. In 774 Charlemagne crowned himself king of Italy.

After returning from Italy, Charlemagne next went to war against the pagan Saxons.

While Charlemagne had been away fighting the Lombards, Saxons had destroyed several Frankish monasteries. Charlemagne vowed to either convert the Saxons to Christianity or to burn Saxony to the ground. Saxon resistance was furious, and Charlemagne's war with the Saxons became a cruel struggle that lasted over thirty years. Early in the war, Charlemagne declared that a Saxon who broke any rule of the church would suffer the death penalty. This strengthened Saxon resolve, and in 782 the Saxons crushed a Frankish army. This so angered Charlemagne that, to punish the rebels, he put to death 4,500 Saxon prisoners. Although the Saxons never again organized a large-scale resistance, rebellions continued until 804.

All during his struggles with the Saxons, Charlemagne continued to fight other wars. In 778 Charlemagne led an army into Spain to aid the Muslim rulers of Barcelona and Saragossa against the Muslim caliph of Cordova. On the way back from Spain, Charlemagne's baggage carriers were massacred by Muslims from Cordova. This incident is the subject of a famous French poem called *Chanson de Roland (The Song of Roland)*.

The New Emperor of the West

Around 795, a chain of events began that would eventually lead to Charlemagne's crowning as emperor of the Romans. In 795, Leo III became pope. Leo came from a very humble family. Because of this, he was hated by the wealthy families of Rome. In 799 Leo was beaten and arrested by agents of these families. Representatives of Charlemagne's government who were visiting Rome freed Leo and brought him to Charlemagne's palace in Aachen (on the present-day border between Belgium and West Germany). While Leo was in Aachen, Frankish church officials probably discussed with Leo the idea of making Charlemagne the new emperor of the west. In the late summer of 800, Charlemagne went with Pope Leo to Rome. When a new rebellion broke out, Charlemagne's son led a Frankish army into Italy. The rebellion was subdued, and the wealthy Romans who had arrested Leo were exiled from Italy. On Christmas Day, in the year 800, Pope Leo crowned Charlemagne as the new emperor of the Romans.

Charlemagne changed Europe not only through his military conquests but in many

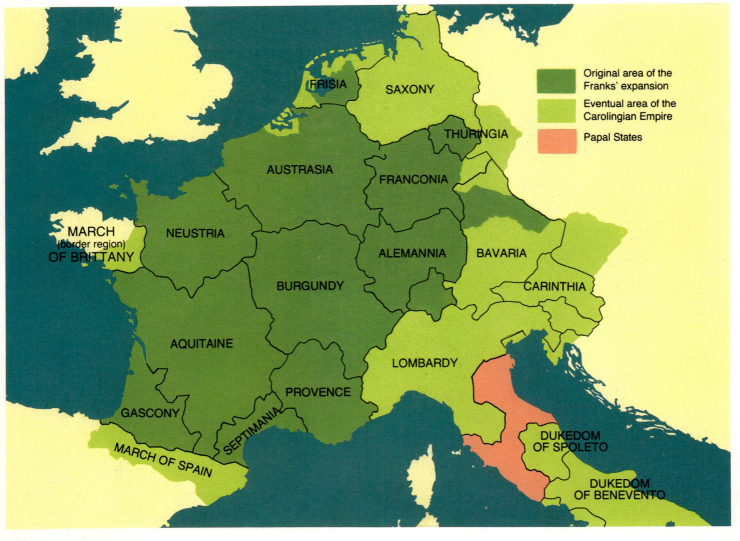

Legend:
- Original area of the Franks' expansion
- Eventual area of the Carolingian Empire
- Papal States

Map labels: FRISIA, SAXONY, THURINGIA, AUSTRASIA, FRANCONIA, MARCH (border region) OF BRITTANY, NEUSTRIA, ALEMANNIA, BAVARIA, BURGUNDY, CARINTHIA, AQUITAINE, LOMBARDY, GASCONY, PROVENCE, SEPTIMANIA, MARCH OF SPAIN, DUKEDOM OF SPOLETO, DUKEDOM OF BENEVENTO

Right: A meeting of Charlemagne with his household officers. Starting in the twelfth or thirteenth century, Charlemagne was portrayed with a full head of hair and a beard, though he was bald and had only a moustache.

other ways. He encouraged reforms in agriculture, education, government, and even art. Charlemagne's practice of rewarding loyal nobles with land in exchange for their military and political services would become the basis of the feudal system in Europe for the next four hundred years.

After Charlemagne died in 814, his empire began to disintegrate. However, Charlemagne's influence upon European civilization would be lasting.

THE EMPIRE OF CHARLEMAGNE

Charlemagne's vision of his empire was to incorporate all of Christendom, including the church, into it. Charlemagne felt that the emperor was the highest power in the land, even higher than the pope.

In order to create an empire in the west governed by a central authority, Charlemagne devised a system. First, he claimed the right to appoint church officials who served in the lands he ruled and who would be loyal to him. He also created an aristocracy consisting of loyal nobles who were given land and government positions. Charlemagne granted the nobles temporary use of the land, called *beneficium,* in exchange for their oath of loyalty. In turn, he encouraged the nobles to obtain oaths of loyalty from the subjects living on the land. The emperor's plan was to extend his influence to all his subjects.

Each year Charlemagne held a general assembly of his governing nobles. The nobles reported to the emperor what was happening in the various regions of the empire. Laws were also made during these assemblies.

To enforce these laws and make sure that the nobles were remaining loyal to him, Charlemagne hired civil officers, called *missi.* The missi traveled in pairs—one church official and one lay person. The missi had the power to unseat a noble from power and withdraw his beneficium if he did not respect Charlemagne's laws.

The Carolingian Renaissance

In 794 Charlemagne established his capital at Aachen. He settled in Aachen because he liked to bathe in the nearby hot springs. His palace was a complex of buildings that covered more than 50 acres (20 hectares). Charlemagne hired the German architect Otto von Metz to design buildings that would be the equal of the Byzantine palaces and churches Charlemagne had seen during his visits to Italy.

Charlemagne had great respect for learning, though he could not read Latin, which was the language of educated people during that time. At Aachen, Charlemagne assembled scholars from all over Europe. He founded a palace school to train both scholars for the church and administrators for his empire. Charlemagne realized that his government officials needed at least a minimal education. He also wanted to establish a common cultural identity within his diverse empire.

Charlemagne appointed an English monk named Alcuin to be the director of his school. Only boys were educated at the palace school, and any boy who showed promise could live at Aachen and attend the school at Charlemagne's expense.

At the palace school, Latin, arithmetic, the Bible, and music were studied. The school scholars also copied classic works from ancient Roman manuscripts. During this time they developed a new style of handwriting, called Carolingian miniscule, which would later be the model for lower-case letters. The cultural and artistic developments during Charlemagne's reign came to be called the Carolingian Renaissance.

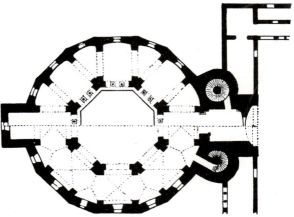

Layout of the Aachen Chapel. The chapel, commissioned by Charlemagne, was built in 805.

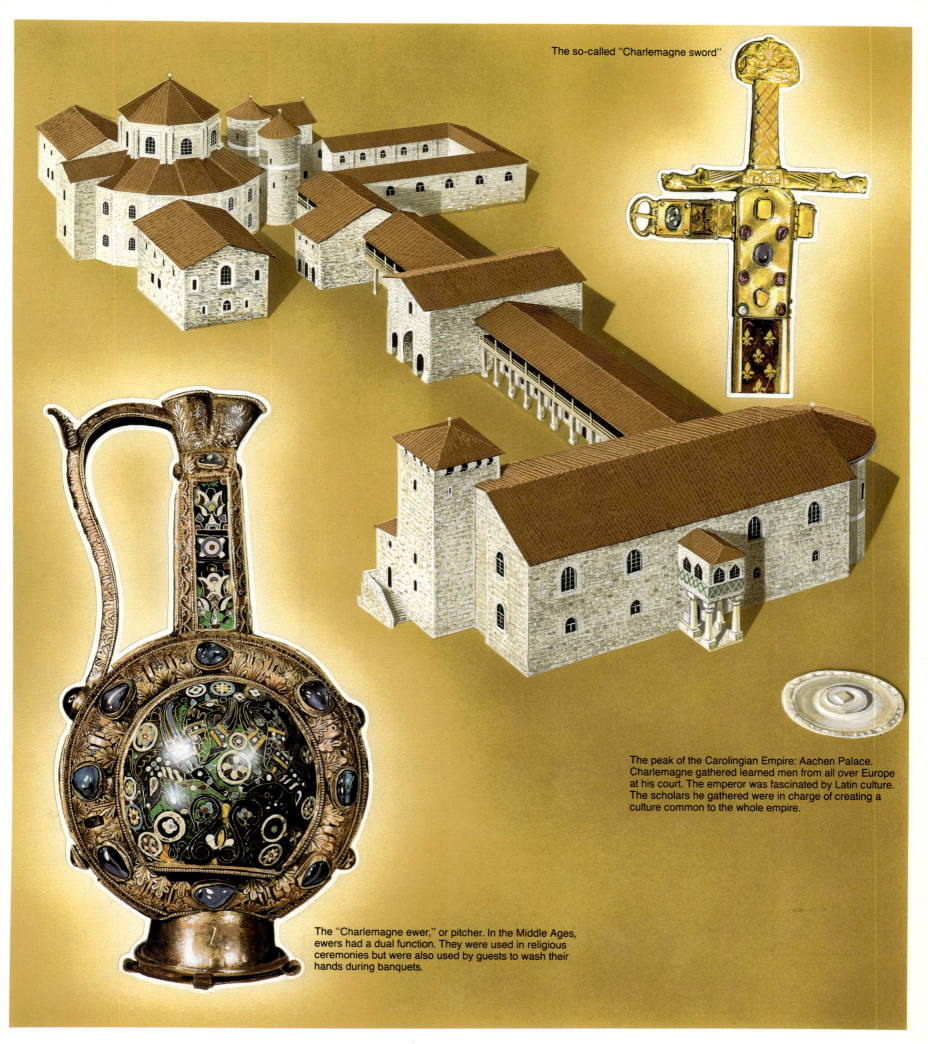

The so-called "Charlemagne sword"

The peak of the Carolingian Empire: Aachen Palace. Charlemagne gathered learned men from all over Europe at his court. The emperor was fascinated by Latin culture. The scholars he gathered were in charge of creating a culture common to the whole empire.

The "Charlemagne ewer," or pitcher. In the Middle Ages, ewers had a dual function. They were used in religious ceremonies but were also used by guests to wash their hands during banquets.

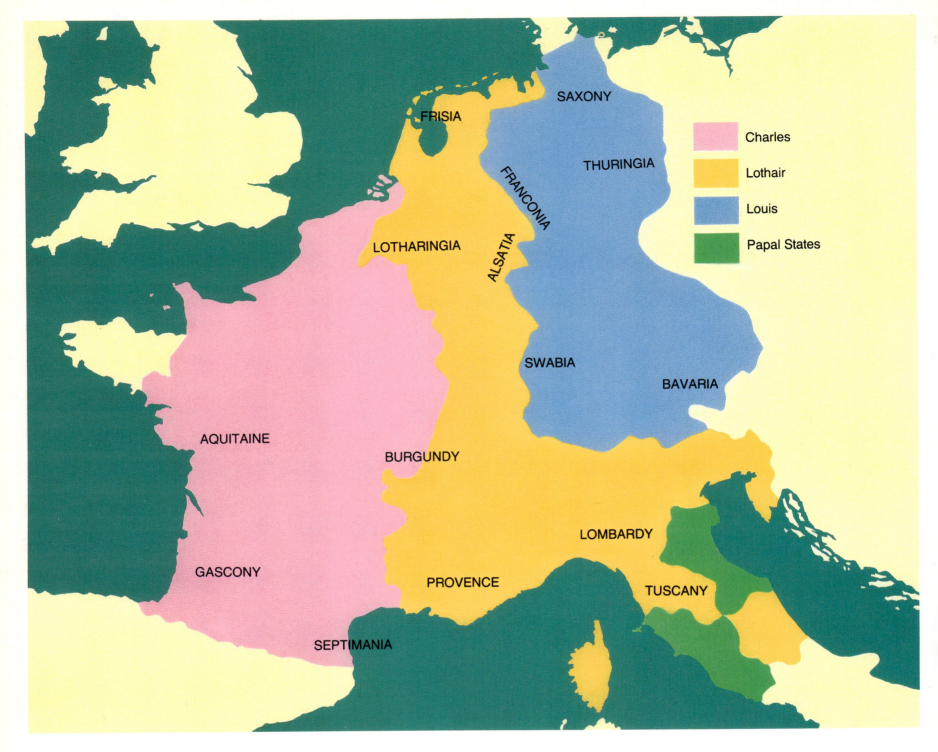

THE DISINTEGRATION OF THE CAROLINGIAN EMPIRE

Shortly before Charlemagne's death in 814, his only surviving legitimate son, Louis the Pious, was crowned emperor. Louis felt differently than his father had about the relationship of the church to the empire. Charlemagne had believed that the emperor had supreme authority, even over the pope. Louis believed that the empire was the highest civil authority but was subject to the pope's spiritual law. Louis was nicknamed "the Pious" because of his devoutness and his interest in church affairs.

Although Louis inherited Charlemagne's empire intact, by the end of Louis's life in 840, the empire had begun to crumble. Louis's downfall was his attempt to divide the empire among his three sons, Lothair, Pepin, and Louis (later called Louis the German). In 817 Louis the Pious proclaimed Lothair co-emperor and gave Aquitaine to Pepin and Bavaria to Louis the German. The sons, however, fought over their lands. In 830 Lothair and his two brothers united to overthrow their father. Louis the Pious regained the throne the following year, but the rest of his life would be filled with struggles with his sons.

In 838 Pepin died, but a fourth son, Charles the Bald, was now included in Louis's inheritance. When Louis the Pious died, Charles and Louis the German formed an alliance against Lothair. The two sides met at the battle of Fontenoy in what is now northern France. Although many soldiers lost their lives, neither side could defeat the other.

The Treaty of Verdun

Unwilling to fight another costly battle, the three brothers signed the Treaty of Verdun in 843. Under this treaty, the empire was divided into three kingdoms. The map on this page shows the borders of these kingdoms. The western kingdom went to Charles the Bald. Lothair ruled the middle kingdom, and Louis the German was

Louis the Pious. The emperor was the last of the Carolingians who reigned over all the territories conquered by Charlemagne.

given the eastern kingdom.

As Charlemagne's heirs died, the kingdoms were divided further. The powerful nobles who served as local rulers gained more and more power and became independent from any central authority. With the empire's decline, the nobles' lands, which had been granted only on a temporary basis by Charlemagne and his heirs, became the private and hereditary property of the nobles. Consequently, the empire broke up into numerous tiny kingdoms, and feudalism became firmly established. Feudalism was a system under which nobles, called vassals, became independent rulers of their own lands, which were called fiefs. A ruler such as a king gave a vassal a fief in exchange for his loyalty and military services. The noble who controlled the fief had economic and political power. He collected taxes on his land, maintained an army of knights, and supervised farming on the fief. The feudal system was based on an agricultural economy. Feudalism would continue in Europe for four centuries.

Charles the Bald (below) and Louis the German formed an alliance against Lothair.

Byzantium was attacked by the Bulgars twice during the tenth century. Emperor Basil II was responsible for the Bulgar defeat in 1014.

BYZANTIUM IN THE NINTH AND TENTH CENTURIES

Basil I

Basil I became the emperor of Byzantium in 867. He had been born in a part of northern Greece called Macedonia and became known as "the Macedonian." Basil had very humble beginnings. He first came to Constantinople as a horse keeper for a wealthy Byzantine family and later worked as a wrestler in a circus. As a wrestler, Basil became very famous. He was hired as a bodyguard for Emperor Michael III and became a trusted friend of the emperor. Soon he was given an important office in the government. However, Basil wanted to be emperor himself. In 866 he convinced Emperor Michael that Caesar Bardas, the highest official in the emperor's government, was a traitor. Michael ordered Basil to murder Caesar Bardas, which Basil was happy to do. As a reward, Emperor Michael named Basil as the heir to the imperial throne. In 867 Basil murdered Michael and became the new emperor.

The Macedonian Emperors

Basil, his son Leo the Wise, and his grandson Constantine VII Porphyrogenitus are known as the Macedonian emperors. Under Leo the Wise, who became emperor in 886, the laws of Byzantium were rewritten. Leo's new law code was called the Basilica. Before the Basilica, Byzantium had been ruled by a set of laws called the Ecloga. The Ecloga had modified the laws of Emperor Justinian in 726. Under the Ecloga, many laws based on old Roman customs were replaced with laws based on Christian beliefs. For example, the laws of Justinian permitted divorce, while the Ecloga prohibited divorce. The Ecloga also forbade the death penalty, except for the most serious crimes. In the Basilica, Leo restored the laws of Justinian and added some new laws of his own.

One serious problem that faced the Macedonian emperors was the power gained by wealthy soldier-farmers. During the early 600s, Byzantine Emperor Heraclius had tried to ease the empire's economic problems by replacing Byzantium's army of soldiers-for-hire with soldier-farmers, who received land in exchange for military service. While this greatly reduced the cost of maintaining an army, it also took direct control of the army away from the emperor. The soldier-farmers commanded their own armies and were able to ignore the wishes of the emperor and do as they pleased. Several times the emperor had to send loyal army units to put down rebellions of the soldier-farmers.

Basil II

Basil II became emperor of Byzantium in 976. Because of his military successes against the Bulgars, Basil was called *Bulgaroktonos* ("killer of Bulgars" in Greek). The Bulgars were a nomadic people from central Asia who had settled in eastern Europe. In 985 the Bulgarian King Samuel began attacking Byzantine lands in Greece. While Basil was busy fighting the Bulgars, a group of powerful soldier-farmers took over parts of Asia Minor (present-day Turkey). By 988 these rebels were threatening Constantinople. Basil was able to defeat the rebels with help from Prince Vladimir, the ruler of the Russian city of Kiev. The Russians and Byzantines had enjoyed friendly relations since the early 900s. After Vladimir's aid to Basil, Basil's sister married Vladimir in 989, and Vladimir and his people accepted the Christian religion of Byzantium.

With the empire's authority restored at home, Basil renewed his war against the Bulgars in 1001. After about four years, Basil had captured more than half of the Bulgarian kingdom. The Bulgars were defeated once and for all at the battle of Syruma, fought in northern Greece in 1014. Basil captured more than fourteen thousand Bulgarian prisoners. He had these prisoners blinded and sent back to their king. It is said that when King Samuel saw the thousands of blind prisoners returning, he became sick and died two days later.

During his rule of almost fifty years, Basil also recaptured many of the Byzantine lands taken by the Muslims. By 999 Byzantine rule had been restored in part of Syria and a large area of what is now Iraq. Although Byzantium would never again rule in northern Italy, Sicily was recaptured from the Muslims by 1043, eighteen years after Basil's death.

The church of Santa Sophia in Kiev in its original form (eleventh century), modeled after Hagia Sophia in Constantinople

Constantine VII is portrayed on this golden coin. This emperor, one of the most educated in Byzantine history, wrote several works about the empire's administration and the tasks of the king.

Viking warrior helmets

Viking silver coins

Greenland

ATLANTIC OCEAN

LABRADOR SEA

NORWEGIAN SEA

Anse-aux-Meadows

Newfoundland

Iceland

Lindisfarne Abbey (monastery) at the end of the eighth century, first victim of the Scandinavian invasions of England

Lindisfarne

Rouen

Elbe River

Seine River

Rhone River

MEDITERRANEAN SEA

The map shows the main lines of Scandinavian expansion. Areas of permanent settlement are marked in red.

The fortified commercial city of Novgorod

THE VIKING CONQUESTS

In the eighth and ninth centuries, the seafaring Scandinavians known as Vikings began sailing to remote lands in search of wealth. The Vikings' ships were shaped like long, shallow canoes and could travel in all types of waterways. Powered by both oars and sail, they moved easily through rivers, lakes, or the open sea. Boatloads of armed Vikings traveled to countries far from Scandinavia. Where the Vikings landed, they attacked peaceful settlements, robbing and killing the inhabitants. Rich monasteries full of gold and silver church decorations—defended only by unarmed monks—were a favorite target of Viking raids.

Vikings from Denmark traveled to western Europe and to the British Isles. In 793 they attacked a monastery on the island of Lindisfarne off the northeast coast of England. By the mid-800s, the Danes ruled almost half the area of England, which they called Danelaw. Some English kings tried to buy peace with the Vikings, but this only encouraged the Vikings to attack more often. During the late 800s, King Alfred of England fought a series of wars against the Vikings. Although Alfred was able to save England from total conquest, the Danes continued to battle the English, off and on, into the eleventh century.

While the Danes were fighting the English, Vikings from Norway were voyaging to the western islands of the North Atlantic. Iceland was first colonized by Vikings around 900. In the 980s, Vikings from Iceland built settlements in Greenland and made voyages to Newfoundland and Labrador in what is now Canada.

Other groups of Vikings moved southward and began attacking lands along the Seine River in France. In 911 the French king gave the Viking leader Rollo a grant of land in exchange for Rollo's promise to help defend the French against other Viking groups. Rollo's Vikings, who became known as Normans, soon adopted the French language and Christian religion. The Norman Vikings later conquered Sicily in 1060 and England in 1066.

While the Vikings were mostly pirates and conquerors, they came as merchants to those areas that were too strong to be conquered. Vikings traveled along the lakes and rivers of eastern Europe to trade with the merchants of Constantinople and Baghdad. Other Vikings settled around the northern cities of Novgorod and Kiev, and quickly took over leadership of the surrounding areas.

Lake Ladoga
Novgorod
BALTIC SEA
Volga River
ARAL SEA
Kiev
Dnieper River
CASPIAN SEA
Golden necklace
Danube River
BLACK SEA
Constantinople
Euphrates River
Baghdad
Persian Gulf

Golden head of a dragon

Casting mold of the tenth century, used to produce small crosses and small hammers of Thor, the Viking god of war

HUNGARIANS AND SARACENS

The Hungarians

The Magyars were a people who came originally from an area in the northern Ural Mountains in what is now the Soviet Union. During the fifth century, one group of Magyars settled around the Don River, just north of the Black Sea. These Magyars called themselves the On-Ogur and would later become known as Hungarians. In the late 800s, a neighboring tribe called the Pechenegs began attacking the Hungarians and drove them westward into Europe. In 889 the Hungarians settled around the Danube River in the area that is present-day Hungary. From there they began raiding neighboring territories. The German regions of Saxony, Bavaria, and Swabia were repeatedly attacked by the Hungarians. They also invaded northern Italy and burned the Italian city of Pavia. The German King Otto I led several campaigns against the Hungarians. In 955 Otto defeated the Hungarians at Lechfeld, near the German city of Augsburg. After this defeat, the Hungarians ended their raids and settled permanently in Hungary.

The Saracens

The Saracens were Muslim pirates who raided Mediterranean seaports and ships during the early Middle Ages. The name *Saracen* comes from *Sarakenos*, which means "easterner" in Greek and was the term that the Byzantines used for all Muslims. From their bases in northern Africa, the Saracens attacked cities on the coasts of France, Italy, Greece, and Asia Minor.

Unlike the Byzantines, the Muslim peoples did not have a history of seafaring. The first recorded naval attack by Muslims was a raid by Muawiya, the Arab governor of Syria, on the Greek island of Cyprus in 649. Muslims soon began battling the Byzantine navy. The Byzantines were defeated in a huge sea battle fought off the southeast coast of Asia Minor in 655. In 698 the Muslims captured Carthage, a Byzantine city on the northern coast of Africa. Carthage became a base for Saracen attacks against the coastal cities of southern Europe. In 827 the Saracens captured the Byzantine-ruled island of Sicily and in 904 attacked Thessalonica in northeastern Greece. By 964 the Saracens also controlled the island of Cyprus.

One group of Saracens settled on the southeast coast of France. These Saracens began raiding deep inland. In 972 this group of Saracens kidnapped a monk named Mailos, who was the abbot of an important French monastery. The monks paid a ransom and Mailos was freed. However, many French nobles considered this kidnapping a crime against the Christian faith. These nobles sent an army to search the Mediterranean coast of France for the Saracens' camp. The army tracked down and killed the Saracen pirates who had seized Mailos. The Italians also had very bitter feelings about the Saracens. After the year 1000, the Italian cities of Amalfi, Pisa, and Genoa successfully fought against the Saracens.

Indirectly, the Saracens had an important effect on the development of Russia. Because of Saracen attacks, many sea traders were afraid to travel through the Mediterranean. Europeans who wanted to trade with Constantinople had to travel along the lakes and rivers of Russia, from the Baltic Sea in the north to the Black Sea in the south. These new trade routes brought great wealth to the cities located on Russia's rivers. The growth of the powerful Russian city of Kiev dates from this period.

Saracen piracy made Mediterranean navigation difficult. The Saracens attacked the cities on the shores and, after looting them, returned to their bases.

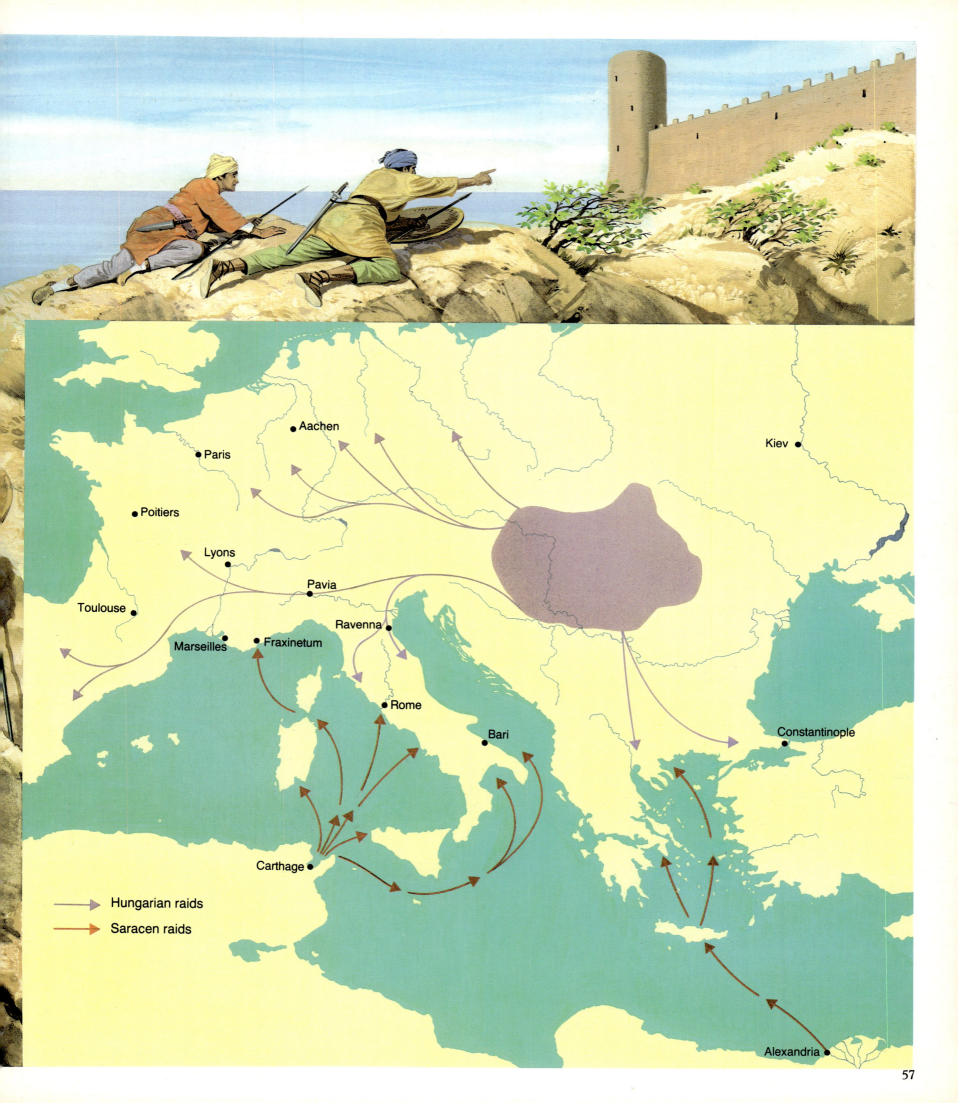

Aachen

Paris

Kiev

Poitiers

Lyons

Toulouse

Pavia

Ravenna

Marseilles

Fraxinetum

Rome

Bari

Constantinople

Carthage

Hungarian raids

Saracen raids

Alexandria

THE FOUNDING OF THE HOLY ROMAN EMPIRE

The Kingdom of France

By the year 887, the division of Charlemagne's great empire was permanent. The former empire consisted of a number of small kingdoms, some of which joined together in loose unions that would eventually became nations. The western Frankish kingdoms would become France. The eastern Frankish kingdoms would become Germany.

In the region of present-day France, the Carolingian kings grew weaker and weaker in power. The local rulers often had more land and wealth than their kings. In 987 the last of the Carolingian kings died. Hugh Capet, one of the local rulers, became the new king. The area of land owned by Hugh himself was small. His possessions consisted only of the Île-de-France, a strip of land between the cities of Paris and Orléans. Rather than expanding their own lands, the descendants of Hugh Capet—known as the Capetian kings—worked to make the local rulers acknowledge the superior authority of the king. Also, each Capetian king made sure, before his own death, to have his son crowned as the new king. As a result of this practice, the crown of France stayed in Hugh Capet's family for more than three centuries.

The Saxon Kings of Germany

In 911 the local rulers of Germany elected as their king Conrad of Franconia (an area located in the southern part of present-day West Germany). Most of Conrad's brief rule was spent fighting Henry of Saxony, who refused to accept Conrad's election. When Conrad died in 919, he left orders that Henry of Saxony should be chosen as the new king. Conrad hoped that this would bring peace to the kingdom. When messengers came to bring Henry the news of his election, Henry was out fowling (hunting with his falcons). Because of this incident, Henry became known as Henry the Fowler. Henry's family—the House of Saxony—would rule Germany for more than one hundred years.

Henry wanted to build a new empire centered in Germany. In 925 Henry captured the French region of Lorraine. Gilbert, the local ruler of Lorraine, married Henry's daughter Gerberga. Henry also built fortresses to protect his kingdom against Hungarian tribes along the kingdom's eastern border. In 935 Henry died following a hunting accident. Henry's son Otto became the new king of Germany. In 936 Otto was crowned in Aachen, the old capital of Charlemagne's empire.

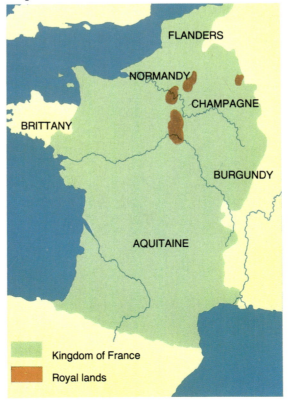

Kingdom of France
Royal lands

Otto I

Like earlier German kings, Otto spent the first years of his rule putting down rebellions. In 939 Otto's uncle Gilbert of Lorraine rebelled against him. King Louis IV of France, who wanted to return Lorraine to French rule, gave aid to Gilbert. Otto's brother Henry also joined the rebels. After a series of battles, the rebels were defeated. Gilbert was killed. Henry, whose life Otto spared, became Otto's most loyal supporter. During these campaigns, Otto carried with him the Holy Lance—a spear said to have pierced the side of Jesus at the crucifixion. Otto believed that this spear gave him God's support for his wars. Otto believed that God wanted him to rebuild the empire of the west.

During this time, the kingdom of Lombardy (the northern area of present-day Italy) was separate from Germany. In 950, King Lothair of Lombardy died. His enemy, Berengar I, was elected king. However, the new king feared that Lothair's widow, Adelaide, would challenge his claim to the throne. Berengar ordered her arrest, but Adelaide escaped to Otto's kingdom and asked Otto for help. Otto sent an army into Italy and defeated Berengar. After marrying Adelaide, Otto himself became king of Lombardy, expanding his kingdom further.

Around 954, Otto's son-in-law, who governed Lombardy for Otto, conspired with Berengar against Otto. At the same time, Hungarian tribes from the east invaded. Otto's army defeated both the Hungarians and the rebels. Otto gave the lands of the rebels to the nobles who had remained loyal, and his kingdom was once again unified.

However, the next year, Otto faced a second invasion from Hungary. At the battle of Lechfeld, fought near the German city of Augsburg,

At the battle of Lechfeld, the army of Otto I defeated the Hungarians.

According to ancient Germanic tradition, the eagle was the symbol of rulers. In the Middle Ages, it became the symbol of imperial authority.

Otto defeated the Hungarians, and his troops proclaimed him emperor. At first, the pope did not accept Otto's claim. The church believed that only the pope had the authority to crown an emperor. However, when Otto's old enemy Berengar invaded the Papal States, Pope John XII turned to Otto for help. After Otto had driven Berengar out of the pope's kingdom, Pope John crowned Otto as emperor on February 2, 962. The empire of Otto came to be called the Holy Roman Empire and would last until 1806.

As emperor, Otto claimed the right to approve the pope. John, who did not want the papacy to be under the emperor's authority, tried to organize a rebellion against Otto. Otto had John arrested and removed from office. Otto replaced John with Leo VII, who was not even a priest. However, Otto soon had to return to Italy with an army when rebellions broke out against Leo. After Leo's death, Otto forced the election of another pope of his choice, John XIII.

In the 960s Otto began a campaign against the remaining Byzantine lands in southern Italy. After making a treaty with the Byzantines, Otto arranged the marriage of his son, Otto II, to the Greek princess Theophano.

Otto II

Otto II became emperor after his father died in 973. Otto II spent the early years of his rule fighting rebellions in Germany and turning back an invasion by the Danish King Harald Bluetooth. In 982 Otto II led an army against the Saracen pirates attacking the coast of By-zantine Italy. However, the Byzantines considered Otto an invader, not an ally. Without the support of the Byzantines, Otto's army was quickly destroyed by the Saracens. Otto died while still in Italy, trying to recruit an army for a second campaign against the Saracens.

Otto III

Otto III was only three years old when his father, Otto II, died in 983. Otto III's mother, Theophano, ruled as Otto's regent until Otto was old enough to rule by himself. Because Otto's father was half Italian and his mother a Byzantine Greek, Otto was more interested in ruling Italy than Germany. Otto wanted Rome to be the capital of both the church and the empire. In 996 Otto moved his residence to Rome. Otto's friend and teacher, Gerbert of Aurillac, was elected as Pope Sylvester II. Otto and Sylvester worked to convert the peoples of eastern Europe. Poland and Hungary both accepted Christianity around the year 1000.

In that year, Otto made a pilgrimage, or religious visit, to the tomb of Charlemagne in Aachen. When Otto returned to Rome, the wealthy Roman families organized a rebellion against him. Otto fled to Ravenna in northern Italy and sent to Germany for an army to help him recapture Rome. In 1002, while still waiting for his army to arrive, Otto died of smallpox. He was twenty-two years old.

The Iberian Peninsula Around the Year 1000

Muslims and Christians

While most of the Iberian Peninsula (present-day Spain and Portugal) was brought under the rule of the Muslims, small Christian kingdoms in the northern mountains were able to resist Muslim rule. Around the year 1000, the Muslim kingdom began to split apart. Arab Muslims and Muslims from northern Africa were often in conflict with each other. Sometimes these conflicts broke out in open war. By the 1030s, Muslim Spain was divided into numerous tiny kingdoms.

While Muslim Spain was divided, the Christian north was becoming more and more prosperous. Around 850, Christians discovered the tomb of James, one of Jesus' first followers and the founder of Christianity in Spain. The church of Santiago de Compostela, built on the site of James's tomb, attracted Christian visitors from all over Europe. The large numbers of religious travelers brought great wealth to the Christian kingdoms. However, the Christian north was slow to unite politically. This was because each Christian king divided up his kingdom among his sons. The kingdoms of the north broke up into smaller and smaller states.

Christian Spain began to be united under Sancho the Great, who became king of Navarre in 1000. Sancho was married to the sister of the ruler of Castile. When Sancho's brother-in-law died, Sancho became the ruler of both Navarre and Castile. Sancho's son Ferdinand I inherited his father's kingdoms. He married the sister of Bermudo III, the ruler of León. When Bermudo died in 1037, Ferdinand added León to his kingdoms.

Other Christian kingdoms continued to fight with each other, however. Some Christian kings even made alliances with Muslim rulers against their fellow Christians. One of the most famous figures of this period was Rodrigo Díaz de Vivar, who was known as El Cid (from *Seid,* a title of respect in Arabic). El Cid was born in the

Many monks from Muslim-controlled areas sought shelter in the northern part of the Iberian Peninsula. The picture shows the abbey of San Pedro de Roda in Catalonia, northern Spain.

northern city of Burgos in 1040 and served first in the army of King Alfonso VI, son of Ferdinand I. However, after he quarreled with Alfonso, El Cid joined the army of the Muslim ruler of Saragossa. When Alfonso VI attacked Valencia, a Christian kingdom allied with Muslim Saragossa, El Cid defeated Alfonso's army. El Cid and his followers then turned against the king of Valencia. El Cid conquered Valencia in 1094 and set up an independent kingdom of his own. In 1102—three years after El Cid's death—Muslims destroyed his kingdom. The heroic deeds of El Cid are recorded in one of Spain's greatest epics, *Poema del Cid*.

Mozarabic Civilization

Mozarabes is the name given to the Christians who lived in the Muslim-ruled part of Spain. These Christians paid a special tax for the right to keep their Christian faith. Most of the Mozarabes lived in Toledo, the old capital of Visigoth Spain. In the early centuries of Muslim rule, the Mozarabes lived in peace with their Muslim and Jewish neighbors. The Christians borrowed many ideas from the Muslims and Jews. This blending of cultures was called the Mozarabic civilization. One way that Mozarabic art expressed itself was in beautifully decorated books produced by Mozarabic monks. Because the Mozarabes were isolated from the Christians living in other parts of Europe, they were not under the authority of the pope. The Mozarabes developed an independent church. Even the Mass performed by the Mozarabes was different from the Mass performed by priests elsewhere in Europe.

In the late eleventh century, after Muslim Spain had broken up into tiny kingdoms, Spain was invaded by a fresh wave of Muslim tribes from Africa. These Muslims were very intolerant of other religions. Many Mozarabes fled to northern Spain to escape persecution by these Muslims. In northern Spain, the Mozarabes merged with the culture of Christian Europe. When Alfonso VI captured Toledo from the Muslims in 1085, the Mozarabic church was brought under the authority of the pope.

THE POLITICAL SITUATION AROUND THE YEAR 1000

The Iberian Peninsula was divided between the Christian kingdoms of the north and the Muslim kingdoms of the south. In the Muslim-ruled areas, a rich civilization resulted from the exchange of ideas among the Christian, Jewish, and Muslim inhabitants.

In England, the Saxons of Wessex fought against invaders from Norway and Denmark.

The Danish King Canute the Great conquered all of England in 1013, but ruled for only about thirty years. By 1043, the Saxons once again ruled England.

Hugh Capet became king of France in 987, though many local rulers had much more power than their king. A group of Vikings who settled in France adopted the French language and

Christian religion. These Vikings were called the Normans.

The new Roman Empire of the west—called the Holy Roman Empire—was created under the German King Otto I. This new empire consisted of Germany and the northern part of Italy. Sicily was ruled by the Muslims, while Byzantium kept its control over southern Italy.

Under Basil II, the Byzantine Empire extended from the Danube River in the north, south to the Tigris River in what is now Iraq. The Bulgar invasion of Greece was pushed back into the Balkans by the Byzantines.

The Slavs from the area of the Dnieper River were united into a kingdom under the Vikings, seafarers from Scandinavia. This kingdom was the beginning of the Russian nation.

After their defeat by the Germans at Lechfeld in 955, the Hungarians settled into the area now known as Hungary.

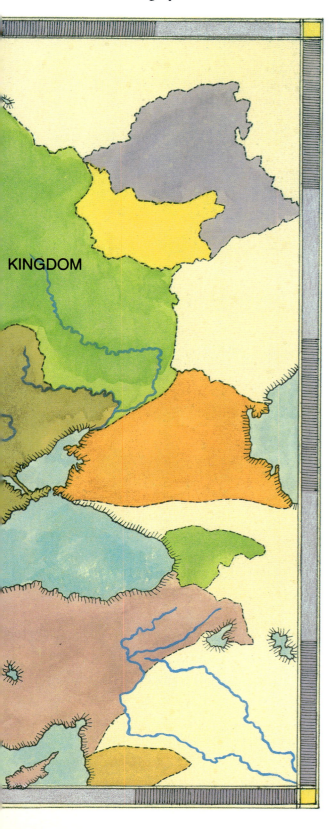

KINGDOM

GLOSSARY

abbot: a man who is head of an abbey (monastery)

alliance: a union formed by mutual agreement, especially to protect or further mutual interests

anchorite: a person who lives apart from others, usually for religious reasons. In the third century, some Christian believers in Egypt withdrew from society to live alone and dedicate themselves to prayer; they were the first anchorites.

barbarian: a person who belongs to a people or a tribe that is not civilized

basilica: an early Christian church having an oblong plan, a high central area separated by columns from aisles at each side, and an apse (recess) at the east end

caliph: the former title of the religious and political leader of some Muslim states

canon law: the body of church rules

cavalry: soldiers who fight on horseback

cenobite: a member of a religious group living together and devoted to prayer. In the fourth century, some Christian believers in Egypt formed small communities; they were the first cenobites and represented the beginnings of true monasticism.

clergy: persons ordained for religious work, such as ministers, priests, and rabbis

doctrine: what is taught as true by a church, nation, or other body

empire: a group of countries or states under one ruler or government

feudal system (or feudalism): the social, economic, and political system of western Europe in the Middle Ages under which people known as vassals gave military service to a king or noble in return for land

fief: in the feudal system, a piece of land given by a king or noble to a vassal, in return for military service

heresy: a religious belief rejected by church authorities as contrary to the established beliefs of the church. A person who believes in a heresy is called a heretic.

hermit: a person who lives apart from others, often for religious reasons

icon: a picture of Christ or other religious figure such as a saint or an angel

iconoclasm: the state of being opposed to worship of images and/or engaging in the act of destroying religious images

illuminated manuscript: a document decorated by hand with gold, silver, colored inks, pictures, and designs

knight: in the Middle Ages, a man raised to an honorable military rank and pledged to do good deeds

Mass: the central service of worship in the Roman Catholic church and in some other churches

medieval: of, having to do with, or belonging to the Middle Ages (between about A.D. 400 and 1500)

monastery: a building or group of buildings where a community of persons, especially monks, live a contemplative life according to fixed rules and under religious vows

monasticism: the condition of living the life of a monk

monk: a man who lives in a monastery as part of a religious community that devotes itself to prayer

mosque: a Muslim place of worship

noble: in the feudal system, a local ruler who was a king's vassal but might control more land than the king

nomad: a member of a group that moves from place to place, usually to find pasture for the group's herd of animals

orthodoxy: a belief or practice that conforms to established doctrine, especially church doctrine

pagan: a person who worships either many gods or no god at all

papacy: the position, rank, or authority of the pope; the term of a pope's rule

papal: of, having to do with, or belonging to the pope

patriarch: a bishop of the highest rank in the early Christian church

penance: a self-punishment or other act done to show sorrow for one's sins or the sins of others

pilgrimage: a journey taken to a sacred or holy place as an act of religious devotion

plague: a disease that is highly contagious, widespread, and often fatal

pope: the supreme head of the Roman Catholic church

renaissance: a new birth; revival

saga: any long narrative story, especially any of the Scandinavian stories of heroic deeds in the Middle Ages

stylite: a monk who lives for years on top of a tall stone pillar, going for days at a time without food or water

theme: in the Byzantine Empire, a large unit consisting of a number of small districts and headed by a supreme military commander

vassal: in the feudal system, a person who held land granted by a king or noble in exchange for providing military service

INDEX

Rothari, King, 25
Rothari's Edict, 25
Rugila, 12, 13
Rule of St. Benedict, 26
Rurik, 35
Rus, 35
Russia, 32, 33, 35, 53, 56, 63

S

saeculares, 19
sagas, 42
Saint Apollinare Nuova, 40
Samuel, King, 53
Sancho the Great, King, 60
sancti, 19
Santiago de Compostela, 60
Saracens, 56, 59
Saragossa, 46, 61
Sardinia, 14
Saxons, 22, 46, 62
Saxony, 56
Scandinavia, 35, 42, 55, 63
Scotland, 22, 23
Scots, 22
Seine River, 55
Serbia, 35
Sergius, 17
Severus, Emperor, 7
Shiites, 30
Sicily, 14, 53, 55, 56, 62
Slavonic, 34
Slavs, 16, 17, 32-33, 34, 35, 63
Somme River, 24
South Saxons, 22
Soviet Union, 56
Spain, 14, 20, 26, 29, 31, 41, 44, 46, 60, 61
Stephen II, Pope, 44
Stephen V, Pope, 34
stylites, 19
Sunna, 30
Sunnites, 30
Sussex, 22
Svarog, 33
Swabians, 10, 20, 56
Sweden, 42
Sylvester II, Pope, 59
Syria, 14, 29, 31, 53

T

taxes, 6, 14, 31, 61
Theodolinda, Queen, 27
Theodora, Empress, 14, 15, 38
Theodoric, King, 39, 40, 41
Theodosius, Emperor, 20
Theophano, Princess, 59
themes, 16
Thessalonica, 56
Thor, 42
Tigris River, 63
Toledo, 20, 31, 61
Toulouse, 20
Trajan, Emperor, 20
Treaty of Verdun, 50
Turkey, 8, 16, 19, 53
Turks, 35, 38

U

Umayyads, 29, 30, 31
Ural Mountains, 56

V

Valencia, 61
Valentinian III, Emperor, 13
Valhalla, 42
Vandals, 10, 14, 20
vassals, 51
Venice, 25